HMS *Eagle* in January 1972, during the final weeks of her operational service. *(Fleet Air Arm Museum)*

HMS EAGLE
1942 – 1978

Neil McCart

FOREWORD BY
REAR-ADMIRAL I. G. W. ROBERTSON CB DSC

To all ex-*Eagles* 1951-1972

Front Cover: A magnificent watercolour painting of the *Eagle* by artist Brian Conroy, Whitehill, Hampshire.

Cover Design by Louise McCart
© Neil McCart/FAN PUBLICATIONS 1996
ISBN: 0 9519538 8 5

Typesetting By: Highlight Type Bureau Ltd,
Clifton House, 2 Clifton Villas,
Bradford, West Yorkshire BD8 7BY

Printing By: The Amadeus Press Ltd,
517 Leeds Road,Huddersfield,
West Yorkshire HD2 1YJ

Published By FAN PUBLICATIONS
17 Wymans Lane, Cheltenham, GL51 9QA, England. Fax & Tel 01242 580290

Contents

Page No.

Foreword by Rear-Admiral I. G. W. Robertson CB DSC 4

Chapter One . . . . .A Royal Launch 5

Chapter Two . . . . .First Commission - Trials & The Home Fleet 11

Chapter Three . . . . . .First Commission - Coronation Review 20

Chapter Four . . . . .First Commission - Mediterranean Fleet 32

Chapter Five . . . . .Second Commission - The First Year 42

Chapter Six . . . . .Second Commission - Operation Musketeer 51

Chapter Seven . . . . . .Third Commission - Return To The Med 63

Chapter Eight . . . . . . .Third Commission - Royal Visitors. 71

Chapter Nine . . . . . . .Fourth Commission - A New Silhouette 83

Chapter Ten . . . . .Fourth Commission - Beira Patrol 94

Chapter Eleven . . . . .Fifth Commission - Withdrawal From Aden 107

Chapter Twelve . . . . .The Sixth - And Final - Commission .120

Chapter Thirteen . . . . .The Sad Demise Of A Proud Ship. .141

Appendix One . . . . . .Principal Particulars 148

Appendix Two . . . . . .Commanding Officers. 149

Appendix Three . . . . .Former *Eagles.* 150

Appendix Four . . . . . .HMS *Eagle* 1913-1942 152

Appendix Five . . . . . .Battle Honours 157

Foreword

It is with much satisfaction that I write this foreword to a narrative of the life of a great ship that has played such an important part in both Royal Navy, and British Maritime, history.

As the last operational Captain of HMS *Eagle*, I have, since giving up my Command of twenty-four years ago, almost every day thought of all those Officers and men who, in modern terms, knew that 'the Company was going into liquidation', yet strove, day and night, to ensure that there was no diminution of the high operational standards set by their predecessors.

These standards saw us through the Falklands War. I hope, and pray, that the present political, and judicial, processes will not erode them for the future.

I am inordinately proud to have served in the Royal Navy, and flown with the Fleet Air Arm, in a whole life's career, and in particular to have played a modest part in this fine aircraft carrier's noble past.

If a ship's motto has real meaning, then this book has certainly shown it.

I. G. W. Robertson CB DSC
Rear-Admiral

Chapter One

A Royal Launch

On 19 May 1942, just eleven days after the Battle of the Coral Sea and as German troops completed the capture of the Kerch Peninsula in the Crimea, a secret letter was dispatched from the Admiralty offices in Bath addressed to the directors of the Belfast shipbuilding company Harland & Wolff Ltd. The letter was headed: 'Fleet Aircraft Carrier', and the first paragraph read: 'I have to request that you will proceed with the construction and completion in all respects of the hull and machinery of one aircraft carrier for HM Navy.' The letter went on to explain that preliminary information regarding the vessel would be ready on Thursday 28 May that same year, and it requested that the company send a representative to the Admiralty offices at Bath in order to discuss the contract, which was numbered CP8/45174/42. Even in those grim days of the Second World War it was clear that the aircraft

The mighty carrier's bow towers over the slipway at Harland & Wolff's Belfast shipyard as preparations are made for the launching ceremony.

(Ulster Folk & Transport Museum)

carrier had superseded the battleship as the Fleet's new capital ship, and the final wording of the letter gives an indication of the importance of the contract: 'The date by which you anticipate that you will be able to give delivery of the vessel should be stated as soon as possible.'

The new aircraft carrier on order from Harland & Wolff had been included in the Admiralty's 1942 building programme and originally it was intended that there would be four ships of the class. The other three orders went to Fairfield's yard on the Clyde, Swan Hunter's on the Tyne and Cammell Laird & Company at Birkenhead. The four ships were to be named HMS *Audacious*, HMS *Africa*, HMS *Eagle* and HMS *Irresistible* respectively. Originally the new vessels were to have been improved versions of the Illustrious-class of aircraft carriers, with a standard displacement of about 27,600 tons, and two full-length hangars. However, in September 1942 it was decided that, with the weight and performance of naval aircraft rapidly increasing, bigger ships were needed and by the time the keel plates for the first of the class were laid on 24 October 1942 at Belfast, the standard displacement tonnage had been increased to 31,600 and the vessel's overall length was set at 790ft, with a beam of 109ft. As originally intended she was to have two full-length aircraft hangars measuring 412ft long and 62ft wide, with a height of 14ft-6in. She would be fitted with two aircraft lifts measuring 45ft by 33ft, and it was envisaged that she would be able to carry at least 72 aircraft. Her main defensive armament would consist of 16, 4·5-inch guns and she would have a speed of over 30 knots. Without doubt, she would be a formidable weapon and the Navy's biggest warship.

The last of the Navy's warships to bear the name *Audacious* was a King George V-class battleship which had been first commissioned in October 1913, for service with the 2nd Battle Squadron of the Home Fleet, but which had fallen victim to a mine off Lough Swilly exactly a year later, on 27 October 1914 - only 12 weeks after the outbreak of the First World War. However, the resurrection of the name was a measure of the new vessel's importance.

When the Second World War ended on 2 September 1945, the *Audacious* was still on the stocks, but she was almost ready for launching and it had already been arranged that she would be christened by HRH Princess Elizabeth. However, with the end of the war it was decided that there was no need for four big fleet carriers of the Audacious class and in October 1945 the order for the *Africa* was cancelled. Three months later, in mid-January 1946, work on the *Eagle*, which had been transferred to

HRH Princess Elizabeth about to pull the launching lever which will send the *Eagle* thundering down the slipway into the Musgrave Channel.

(Ulster Folk & Transport Museum)

Vickers Armstrong's shipyard at Walker-on-Tyne, was stopped when that contract was also cancelled. The men who had been working on the ship were transferred to merchant ships which were under construction or being refitted at the shipyard, for the rebuilding of the nation's decimated merchant fleet now took priority over naval vessels. There had been changes too at Cammell Laird's Birkenhead shipyard where the *Irresistible* had been renamed *Ark Royal*, to commemorate her namesake which had been lost to a U-boat's torpedo on 14 November 1941. Finally, at the end of January 1946, the *Audacious* was renamed *Eagle*, in honour of her predecessor which had been torpedoed and sunk in the Mediterranean on 11 August 1942, with the loss of 160 lives.

The launch of the *Eagle* was set for Tuesday 19 March 1946 and, although the launch of a great ship was always

cause for celebration in Belfast, this was a very special occasion for the city and its people for it marked a visit by HRH Princess Elizabeth. Two days earlier, on Sunday 17 March, the Princess had travelled north by train from London to Greenock where she embarked in the cruiser *Superb* for the crossing to Belfast. The following day, after a rough passage, the *Superb*, escorted by the destroyers *Fame* and *Hotspur*, arrived off the Pile Lighthouse and the royal party trans-shipped to HMS *Fame* which secured alongside the city's Dufferin Dock at 5.15pm on Monday 18 March.

The dawn of Tuesday 19 March 1946 brought a wet day, with thick clouds and steady rainfall, but the inclement weather did not deter the crowds who lined the route to Harland & Wolff's Musgrave Yard where there were thousands more people to witness the ceremony. In

At 11.30am on Tuesday 19 March 1946 HMS *Eagle* entered the water for the first time. (*Ulster Folk & Transport Museum*)

HMS *Eagle* anchored in Bangor Bay in late October 1951, shortly before she was provisionally accepted into service with the Royal Navy. She is flying the Harland & Wolff houseflag at her masthead and the Red Ensign at the stern.

(Ulster Folk & Transport Museum)

the shipyard itself work had come to a standstill as the workmen and their families gathered in force, while over the whole scene towered the *Eagle's* massive grey bulk, with her smoothly welded sides. So great was her beam that there seemed to be only inches between her and the gantries on either side. Below her bows stood the royal launching platform which was draped in red, white and blue, with a bottle of Australian wine poised for its short swing against the ship's stem. From the openings in the ship's side workmen peered down on the slipway where, under the bulbous bottom of the *Eagle's* hull, last minute clearing and preparation of the slipway was feverishly being carried out. Nearby other stands had been built for the band, choir, official guests and the Press photographers, whilst on the ground and at every vantage point, spectators were massed. Some of the bolder spirits had even climbed up onto the cranes where they appeared to be perched very precariously over the slipway.

That morning, as HRH Princess Elizabeth drove from Government House at Hillsborough, the rain stopped and when the royal party arrived at the main offices of Harland & Wolff they were received by Sir Frederick Rebbeck, the chairman and managing director of the shipbuilding company. After the initial formalities the Princess was driven to the launching platform where the Band of the Royal Inniskilling Fusiliers played the National Anthem, and she inspected a Guard of Honour and a contingent of Sea Rangers. Just before she ascended the launching platform, the Princess was presented with a bouquet by 17-

year-old James Christian, the youngest of Harland & Wolff's apprentice shipwrights. At 11.20am, as workmen began to hammer out the wooden chocks under the stem of the ship and anxious shipyard managers stationed by the launching cradles watched for any movement of the hull, the short religious ceremony began.

The Rector of Ballymacarrett read the 105th Psalm, 'They that go down to the sea in ships and occupy their business in great waters...' This was followed by the prayer 'O Thou that sittest above the water floods and stillest the raging of the seas...' which was spoken to the accompaniment of the final blows of the hammers down below on the slipway. Then, led by the Queen's Island Choir and the Band of the Royal Irish Fusiliers, the great crowd which had assembled joined in the moving hymn of the sea, 'Eternal Father Strong To Save', and as the last strains of the music died away the Benediction was given and a silence fell over the whole shipyard.

At 11.40am precisely HRH Princess Elizabeth stepped forward and, taking the bottle of wine in both hands, she sent it crashing against the bows of the ship, declaring, 'I name this ship *Eagle*. May God protect her and all who sail in her.' Before she had finished speaking, the ship started to move down the slipway and the band's rendition of 'Rule Britannia' was almost drowned by the cheers of the shipyard workers as they saw the massive hull thunder down the slipway into the smooth waters of the Musgrave Channel, which had been specially dredged for the occasion.

Once in the water her movement was soon stopped and the waiting tugs brought her under control, whilst overhead a flight of 12 Seafires from RNAS Eglinton roared past and dipped in salute over the ship. As HRH Princess Elizabeth and the official guests made their way back to the company's offices, the *Eagle* was towed round to the east side of the Thompson Wharf where she was laid up and placed in the care of a small maintenance party. In the yard itself work was resumed and on the *Eagle's* vacant slipway the first keel plates of a 27,000-ton liner, which was to be built for the Union Castle Line, were laid.

Meanwhile at the official luncheon which followed the *Eagle's* launching, the toast 'HMS *Eagle*' was proposed by Sir Basil Brooke, the Prime Minister of Northern Ireland, and in response Admiral of the Fleet Lord Cunningham recalled that Captain Cook, as an able seaman, and Lord Rodney, as a captain, had served in the eighth *Eagle*. He went on to say that the last HMS *Eagle* was the first aircraft carrier to work with the fleet in battle, and that she was the first carrier to provide fighter protection for the fleet. It was also interesting to note that this new *Eagle* was the sixth aircraft carrier to be built for the Royal Navy by Harland & Wolff, and their 91st warship.

As a memento of the occasion, Sir Basil Brooke presented HRH Princess Elizabeth with a diamond brooch in the shape of an eagle, and in her speech to those assembled the Princess said: 'A short while ago we watched a most stirring spectacle, as a great ship, as yet incomplete but nevertheless a triumph of British design and shipbuilding, was released from her cradle on dry land and moved gracefully down to her natural element, the sea. There is something deeply stirring about the launching of a ship, but for us, an island race with centuries of seafaring tradition in our blood, there is a special significance in that moment when she starts to move from the stocks which stirs our national pride in a way which, I am sure, cannot be understood by the peoples of those countries to whom the sea is only of secondary importance.'

The Princess went on to pay a tribute to Harland & Wolff: 'Of the many shipbuilding firms which have grown up around the coasts, none has won greater worldwide fame than the firm of Harland & Wolff. The large number of ships which they have built for foreign countries is in itself the proof of their international reputation. Your ships have not only been designed by the finest brains of marine engineering but every minute operation in their vast and complex construction has been effected by men and women who are not only expert at their craft but who inherit through countless generations a love and devotion for their trade. I am sure that the enthusiasm of the thousands of men and women who built a fine ship like the *Eagle* will be kept alive by the men who will sail her upon the seven seas.'

After referring to the last HMS *Eagle*, which was originally built as a battleship and later converted into an aircraft carrier, Her Royal Highness said: 'The *Eagle* we have seen launched today never had any doubts in her mind. From her earliest moments she was determined to be the greatest and most modern aircraft carrier afloat.' After paying tribute to the Fleet Air Arm the Princess wished good fortune to the men who would fly off the decks of the *Eagle*, and she expressed the hope that the ship would be a great and magnificent addition to the fleet. It had been a resoundingly successful day, but it would be more than five years before the *Eagle* became an operational unit of the Royal Navy.

The *Eagle* was laid up for almost a year before work began, during 1948, to fit her out. By that date a number of improvements to the accommodation for the ship's company had been introduced. The most significant of these was probably the fitting of an American-style self-service cafeteria. This messing system had first been used in British ships during the war when large numbers of US-built vessels had come to the Royal Navy under the Lend-Lease scheme. The centralized arrangement had proved to be very popular and in the *Eagle* there were two large dining halls on 2 Deck forward, which would operate two sittings to cater for the large numbers involved. The dining hall for Chiefs and Petty Officers was situated on 5 Deck forward, but the system by which meals were collected at a servery and taken the short distance to the dining hall was the same. Everyone welcomed the new arrangement as it did away with mealtimes being spent in mess decks which, in effect, became recreation and sleeping spaces. Some thought was also given to the fitting of standee bunks in the mess decks, but it was decided that hammocks were more practical and so they were retained.

On Thursday 27 May 1949, Her Royal Highness Princess Elizabeth, accompanied by the Duke of Edinburgh, again visited Belfast and during the afternoon they visited Harland & Wolff's shipyard where they were given a guided tour of the *Eagle* which was berthed alongside Thompson Wharf.

On 7 March 1951, as the task of fitting out the new carrier neared completion, her first commanding officer, Captain Guy Willoughby RN, was appointed, together with a number of key personnel. In late October 1951 *Eagle* underwent the contractor's sea trials, and by the last day of the month she was ready to undergo her acceptance trials. She was actually handed over to Captain Willoughby on Wednesday 31 October 1951 in Bangor Bay. The ship stopped in a position Lat 54° - 48'N/Long 05° - 26'W, where Vice-Admiral Sir Denis Maxwell KCB CBE, Engineer-in-Chief of the Fleet, provisionally accepted HMS *Eagle* from Harland & Wolff and Captain Willoughby took command.

Ron Lewis, who was a telegraphist at that time, recalls his first impressions of the *Eagle*: 'In October 1951 I was serving at the RN Signal School at St Budeaux and whilst I was there I was promoted to Leading Telegraphist and drafted to HMS *Eagle* at Belfast. I can remember that it was an arduous journey by train from Plymouth to Liverpool, and then by the overnight ferry over a rough Irish Sea to Belfast. It seemed to me that just about everyone on the ferry, apart from myself, was seasick and it was a great relief to arrive in Belfast. That same day I joined the *Eagle*, which was anchored in Bangor Bay, and within hours of my arrival the ship was commissioned and handed over to Captain Willoughby by the builders. Soon after I arrived on board I ran into an old shipmate, Francis "Chats" Harris, a leading cook. We had been in the old minesweeper HMS *Sylvia* together and, after working in a galley which was only a few feet square, he was delighted with his duties in the spacious bakery on board the *Eagle*.'

Following her acceptance by Captain Willoughby, *Eagle* got under way and at 1.15pm on the last day of October 1951, with the ship's company mustered on the flight deck, the Red Ensign was hauled down and the White Ensign was hoisted. HMS *Eagle* became the newest and the biggest warship in the Royal Navy.

On the afternoon of Tuesday 27 November 1951, as *Eagle* rounded Land's End in driving rain, a Sea Fury from RNAS Culdrose took a series of photographs of the ship.

(R. Lewis)

Chapter Two

First Commission - Trials & The Home Fleet

At the conclusion of the handing over ceremonies, the *Eagle* anchored once again in Bangor Bay and remained there for three days. On the afternoon of Friday 2 November 1951 an official visit was made to the ship by the Prime Minister of Northern Ireland and at 4pm the next day she weighed anchor and courses were set for Plymouth. Her passage down the Irish Sea was undertaken at only moderate speed so that all the ship's company, and particularly the engine room department, could get used to handling the ship, and at 8pm on Sunday 4 November she was abeam of Bishop Rock as she rounded the Isles of Scilly. However, with high winds, driving rain and poor visibility it is doubtful whether her progress was noted by anyone on shore. That night she steamed up the Channel and at 9.30am on Monday 5 November she passed the breakwater and entered Plymouth Sound for the first time. However, with the weather having deteriorated still further, it was decided that she would not proceed up-harbour that day and the new carrier was secured to C buoy, off Picklecombe Point, a berth which was to become very familiar to the ship over the next 21 years. Next day it was hoped that she could proceed alongside and, at just after 8am, Special Sea Dutymen were piped to their stations, but with high winds, heavy rain and continued poor visibility it was decided to remain at C buoy for a further 24 hours. Finally, at 10.25am on Wednesday 7 November, *Eagle* slipped her moorings and, without any ceremony, steamed the final few miles up-harbour and, just over an hour later, she secured alongside 6 & 7 berths of Devonport Dockyard.

During the following few days stores were embarked, and on the afternoon of Sunday 11 November the ship was opened to the public who naturally took a great interest in the Navy's new aircraft carrier. At 1.45pm the next day, again without any ceremony, the *Eagle* left her berth and later in the afternoon she was again secured to C buoy in the Sound. On the following morning the lower deck was cleared and at 9.40am the C-in-C Plymouth embarked to inspect Ceremonial Divisions which, because of inclement weather, were held in the upper hangar. Finally, at 4pm on Wednesday 14 November 1951, the *Eagle* left Plymouth Sound for the Firth of Clyde where her trials were to be carried out.

It was 5pm on Saturday 17 November 1951 when the *Eagle* anchored off Greenock and at 9.30am the next day she weighed anchor for speed trials off the measured mile at Arran. During the next week the *Eagle* became a familiar sight as she weighed anchor in the early morning to put to sea for trials, and arrived back off Greenock each

evening to anchor for the night.

One man who recalls seeing the *Eagle* at this time, and later served in her as a Petty Officer Electrician, was Michael Pack: 'My first association with the *Eagle* was in November 1951 when she was undertaking her trials in the Firth of Clyde. I was serving in the elderly boom defence vessel, HMS *Barrington*, and we were engaged in lifting the boom between Dunoon and Cloch Point which had been part of the Clyde's wartime defences. The *Barrington* was actually a coal burner which had seen "better days" and, as the only electrician on board, I used to assist the stokers to trim the coal in the bunkers and the furnaces.

During her trials the *Eagle* used to anchor regularly each evening off Helensburgh and each morning she would leave the Clyde for her trials. One morning, as we shovelled all the coal dust and all the ship's rubbish into our furnaces and, as usual, thick, black, greasy smoke belched from our funnel, we received a signal from the immaculate looking aircraft carrier, which was the pride of the Royal Navy, requesting, "Will you please make less smoke. You are spoiling my new paintwork." Needless to say, after that, our coal dust and rubbish was stoked into the furnaces much earlier, and before the *Eagle* got under way.'

On Wednesday 21 November, shortly before the *Eagle* sailed for her manoeuvrability trials off Ailsa Craig, Press representatives were embarked for a day at sea in the more open waters south of Arran. These trials were designed to establish the *Eagle's* turning circles at different speeds with varying degrees of rudder. Of considerable importance was the assessment of pressures exerted on the ship's twin balanced rudders when they were put hard over at speed. On the last day of her trials, as the ship was put through her paces at full power, six Firefly FR5 aircraft from RNAS Eglinton carried out dummy attacks on the carrier. Throughout the next day, Saturday 24 November, the *Eagle* remained at anchor off Greenock refuelling and on Sunday, after Divisions, the ship's company were finally able to relax after six demanding days.

At 9.35am on Monday 26 November 1951 the *Eagle* weighed anchor once again and steamed south with courses set for Spithead where she would start her flying trials and work-up off the south coast. Once again her voyage was made through rough seas and driving rain, but this did not prevent a Sea Fury from RNAS Culdrose from flying over the ship and taking a series of photographs of the *Eagle* as she rounded Land's End and entered the Channel. Less than 24 hours later, at 8am on Wednesday 28 November 1951, the carrier was off the Nab Tower and three hours

This view of the *Eagle* taken on 27 November 1951 shows her flight deck as originally constructed. At that time her flight deck code was J.
(Fleet Air Arm Museum)

HMS *Eagle* anchored at Spithead in March 1952. Parked on the after end of the flight deck are three Firebrand torpedo/strike aircraft of 827 Squadron, which were phased out of service that year. *(M. K. Pagan)*

At anchor in Spithead. (*M. K. Pagan*)

later she anchored at Spithead.

The *Eagle* remained in the area for five days, and during this time Captain Willoughby called on the C-in-C Portsmouth and, as there was a great deal of public interest in the ship, during the afternoon of Sunday 2 December she was opened to visitors who were ferried out to her by tenders. The next day, Monday 3 December 1951, was a landmark in the *Eagle's* career. After weighing anchor at 9.15am, she steamed to an exercise area south of the Isle of Wight where 'Flying Stations' was piped for the first time and Lieutenant S. A. Mearns RN became the first pilot to take off from the *Eagle's* 800ft flight deck, when he was launched in an Avenger which had been embarked by lighter. Following this *Eagle* carried out gunnery and radar calibration trials and finally, on the morning of Friday 14 December 1951, she left the Solent for Plymouth Sound. That same evening she secured to C buoy and six days later she proceeded up-harbour to berth alongside 5 & 6 wharves of Devonport Dockyard.

On Wednesday 19 December 1951, as the *Eagle* berthed alongside at Devonport Dockyard, the invoice from her builders for £11,642,000 for the construction of the carrier was received at the Admiralty offices in Bath. At the Admiralty's request the total cost was broken down and this showed that £7,662,000 was for the construction of the hull, £2,620,000 was for the main propulsion machinery and the auxiliary machinery and £1,360,000 was for the fitting of the ship's electrical machinery and wiring.

Back on board the *Eagle* the starboard watch leave party were preparing to depart for the Christmas break, whilst those remaining carried on with routine maintenance. On 25 December, after a carol service in the upper hangar, the 'Pipe Down' was sounded and three days later, as the starboard watch returned on board and the port watch took

their leave, the *Eagle* played host to the BBC for a live broadcast of the popular radio show 'Any Questions', which was held in the lower hangar.

The New Year was ushered in when 16 bells were struck and a children's party was held in the lower hangar, but it was not long before work had to start in earnest and at 1pm on Wednesday 23 January, the *Eagle* left her berth for the Sound where she was moored to C buoy for 21 days. This is where she was on Wednesday 6 February 1952 when HRH King George VI died at Sandringham. At 11.30am that day Captain Willoughby read the proclamation of the accession of Queen Elizabeth II, after which a gun salute was fired and at midday the colours were lowered to half mast as a mark of respect for the late King.

The next afternoon the *Eagle* left Plymouth Sound bound, once again, for the Solent where her flying trials were to take place. These started at 7.45am on Thursday 14 February when the ship went to 'Flying Stations' and 20 minutes later the first two aircraft, two Avengers from RNAS Ford, arrived overhead and landed safely. At 10.22am the first Avenger was catapulted and for the remainder of that day, and throughout the following two weeks, the trials continued in earnest as a succession of Avengers, Sea Furies, Firebrands and Sea Hornets landed

A dramatic view of an Attacker landing on *Eagle's* flight deck in June 1952. Note that the pilot is being guided in by the Deck Landing Control Officer or 'batsman'.

(*Fleet Air Arm Museum*)

An Attacker makes an emergency landing into the crash barrier during flying trials in June 1952. *(Fleet Air Arm Museum)*

A Firebrand of 827 Squadron crash lands during the flying trials of June 1952.

(G. Austin)

Two mishaps during 'Exercise Main Brace' in September 1952. An Attacker which appears to be beyond repair, and...

...a Firebrand is caught by the barrier.
(G. Austin)

A US Navy helicopter bringing NATO officers to the debriefing which followed 'Exercise Main Brace'. The *Eagle* is anchored in Oslofjord. *(Fleet Air Arm Museum)*

on and took off from the *Eagle's* flight deck. Being the largest aircraft carrier in the Royal Navy the *Eagle* was capable of handling bigger and faster aircraft than any previous carrier, including, of course, jet aircraft. The first one to land and take off from the *Eagle* was a Sea Vampire F20, during the afternoon of Thursday 21 February. However, it would not be Sea Vampire squadrons which would use the *Eagle* operationally, but the rather ungainly-looking Supermarine Attackers, the first of which landed on the carrier during the afternoon of 28 February 1952.

During the first phase of her flying trials the *Eagle* had been anchoring each evening in Sandown Bay or at Spithead but on the afternoon of Friday 29 February she entered Portsmouth Harbour and secured alongside South Railway Jetty for a long weekend, before embarking her squadrons. During this weekend at Portsmouth the *Eagle* was, once again, opened to the public and within the space of only four hours thousands of people came to the dockyard to visit the ship. However, on the morning of Monday 3 March 1952 it was back to work again as the

personnel of 800 (Attacker) and 827 (Firebrand) Squadrons were embarked. Later that day the *Eagle* slipped her berth and left Portsmouth Harbour to anchor at Spithead for the night. Next morning, at 9am, she weighed anchor and put to sea where the aircraft of both 800 and 827 Squadrons were landed on without incident. There then followed nine days of intensive flying exercises in the Channel, with the ship steaming as far west as the Channel Islands on one occasion. On two days during her flying trials the Deputy Chief of Naval Staff was embarked in the ship to observe her and her aircraft being put through their paces. George Austin, who was serving with 800 Squadron remembers that, 'It was very easy to get lost on board the *Eagle* and we were given a small map showing the ship's layout. In addition, if you did get lost, you could always ring the switchboard and they would give instructions on how to find your way back to your mess deck area.'

HMS *Eagle's* final acceptance as an operational unit of the Royal Navy was marked by a Service of Dedication which was held in the lower hangar during the morning of

Sunday 16 March 1952, whilst the ship was anchored at Spithead. The service was conducted by the Venerable L. Coulshaw, the Chaplain of the Fleet, who told the assembled ship's company that the Queen, who had launched the ship at Belfast six years earlier, had always taken a special interest in the *Eagle* and that, had it not been for her recent accession to the throne, she would have attended the service that day. After dedicating the ship's chapel to St John The Evangelist, the service was concluded and HMS *Eagle* was accepted into the Home Fleet.

The *Eagle* then put to sea again for further trials in the Channel, during which 800 Squadron's Attackers were dispatched from the ship's two hydraulic catapults at intervals of just under one and a half minutes. Although this was not as fast as it would be done later in the commission, it demonstrated the skill with which the ship's company were handling the new vessel. During the exercises both the Attackers and the Firebrands made dummy attacks on the ship, and they also provided the radar teams and the gun crews with realistic training conditions. However, the fast pace of technical progress in naval aviation made it clear, even at this early stage, that the hydraulic catapults would need to be replaced by the new steam catapult which was being developed. Unfortunately the trials were cut short on the last day because of thick fog and on the morning of Friday 21 March *Eagle* returned to Portsmouth Harbour and secured alongside South Railway Jetty. This was another weekend visit and during the short stay she received on board the Second Sea Lord Vice-Admiral Sir Alexander Madden KCB, as well as being opened to the public. After leaving Portsmouth during the morning of Monday 24 March 1952, the *Eagle* set courses for Portland where she took part in fleet gunnery exercises before securing alongside 5 & 6 berths in Devonport Dockyard on 27 March.

It was Thursday 15 May 1952 before the *Eagle* put to sea again, and three days were spent at C buoy in Plymouth Sound carrying out trials on her flight deck barrier. Following this she steamed east to the exercise area south of the Isle of Wight for her next series of flying trials. This time, however, she operated with a Fairey Gannet prototype and Sea Hawk aircraft, neither of which had been accepted into service at that stage. After spending a long weekend anchored at Spithead the *Eagle* put to sea again, this time to make aviation history. During the morning of Wednesday 28 May 1952, whilst south of the Isle of Wight, a Vickers Supermarine 508 flown by Mr M. J. Lithgow, a Supermarine test pilot, successfully made its first deck landing on an aircraft carrier. The following morning the same aircraft was safely launched and later in the day the *Eagle* was to be seen alongside Portsmouth Dockyard's South Railway Jetty again. The Supermarine 508 was considered, at that time, to be the most powerful naval fighter in the world and this butterfly-tailed

prototype, much modified, eventually became the remarkable and good-looking Scimitar F1 fighter.

After another long weekend alongside at Portsmouth, the *Eagle* sailed again on the morning of Wednesday 4 June and next day the Attackers of 803 and 820 Squadrons and the Firebrands of 827 Squadron landed before the *Eagle* anchored at Spithead for the night. At 11am on Friday 6 June the new carrier weighed anchor and, in company with the destroyer *Ulysses*, she set courses for the Moray Firth by way of the Irish Sea and the Pentland Firth. Finally, on the evening of Tuesday 10 June 1952 the *Eagle* joined the battleship HMS *Vanguard*, and other units of the Home Fleet, for exercises off the north-east coast of Scotland. On Friday 20 June 1952, the First Lord of the Admiralty, the Secretary of State for Air and the Minister of Supply flew on board ship in two Avengers to view an impressive flying display by the two squadrons of Attackers, after which the *Eagle* anchored off Lossiemouth for a weekend of relaxation. The flying exercises with the fleet continued throughout the following week, after which some time was spent at anchor off Rosyth. During the first weekend in July the *Eagle* returned to the Solent area for another week of flying exercises in the Channel south of the Isle of Wight. This initial phase in the *Eagle's* career was concluded on Monday 14 July 1952 when she slipped her moorings at C buoy in Plymouth Sound, where she had spent the weekend, and with full ceremony she steamed into harbour and berthed alongside 5 & 6 wharves of Devonport Dockyard. Two weeks later she was moved into No 10 dry dock for routine maintenance before she sailed once again, this time for NATO's autumn exercises in northern waters off the coast of Norway.

During August Rear-Admiral J. Hughes-Hallet, Flag Officer Heavy Squadron, hoisted his flag in the *Eagle* and on 1 September 1952 the personnel of 800, 803, 814, 827 and 849 Squadrons joined the ship. One of those who joined the *Eagle* at that time was Terry Heaps, an aircraft handler, who recalls the experience: 'She was the biggest carrier at that time and I found that it was difficult getting to know people. On our mess deck alone, 63 Mess, there were 77 aircraft handlers who were employed in the hangars. One very nice feature of the *Eagle* was the cafeteria messing, which was far better than the mess deck system I had experienced on board the *Illustrious*.'

Next day, at 4.30pm, the *Eagle* put to sea and steamed up Channel to embark her aircraft, before turning round and setting courses for Greenock by way of the Irish Sea. Sunday 7 September was the last day of calm, sunny weather and after Divisions on the flight deck, which were inspected by FOHS whilst the ship was abeam of Bishop Rock, the *Eagle* rendezvoused with the *Illustrious*, the cruiser *Swiftsure*, and the destroyers *Ulster* and *Aisne*. All the ships then steamed north to Greenock to join the remainder of the Home Fleet, which included the battleship *Vanguard*, flying the flag of the C-in-C Home Fleet Admiral Sir George Creasy KCB CBE DSO, and a US Navy task force led by the Iowa-class battleship USS *Wisconsin,* flying the flag of Vice-Admiral Stump USN.

'Exercise Main Brace' started on Saturday 13 September 1952 when, in the early hours of the morning, the NATO fleet left its anchorage off Greenock and steamed north of the Arctic Circle where the already poor weather conditions continued to deteriorate still further. This was the *Eagle's* first opportunity to play a fully operational role with the Home Fleet, and 'Main Brace' was a massive exercise involving the ships of eight nations. However, the weather was no respecter of NATO plans, and two days into the exercise all the *Eagle's* and *Illustrious'* flying operations were abandoned because of heavy seas and storm force winds. During the evening of 17 September most of the *Eagle's* carley floats were lost overboard and it was Sunday 21 September before the storms had abated enough to allow flying to recommence. At 5.50pm that day, off North Jutland, the Dutch destroyer *Van Galen* closed the *Eagle's* starboard side in order to take on fuel and, despite the heavy seas, the hoses were connected. However, at just after 6.30pm, the *Van Galen* suddenly veered to port and collided with the *Eagle* abreast the Blacksmith's Shop on 4 Deck. Her stem actually holed the carrier's hull, but fortunately no one was injured. All the fuelling gear was lost and the *Van Galen's* stem and forecastle were damaged, which meant that the destroyer had to return to harbour for repairs, but in the event the *Eagle's* operations were not affected.

Ron Lewis' memories of 'Exercise Main Brace' are of, '...the beautiful sunrises and the sight of ice-covered hawsers and handrails on the weather decks. I still have my "bluenose" certificate which commemorated our service in the Arctic Circle. It was signed by Lt-Cdr J. D. Jackson, our Communications Officer, whom we knew affectionately as "Jacko".'

The exercise ended officially at 7pm on Tuesday 23 September 1952, and at 11am the next day the combined fleet anchored in Oslofjord just outside the Norwegian capital city. During the morning of Saturday 27 September a conference was held in the *Eagle's* upper hangar to discuss lessons learned during the exercise. This was attended by not only the NATO commanders, but also by His Majesty King Haakon and Crown Prince Olav of Norway. The critique lasted for about three hours and on its conclusion Lord Ismay, the NATO Secretary General, issued the following statement: 'We are highly satisfied with the manner in which "Main Brace" has been planned and executed; the exercise not only offered an outstanding opportunity for international cooperation, but also provided practice in tactical and strategic coordination between the NATO commands. A test of this sort enables us to determine our weaknesses and the corrective measures which we must take.'

However, for the ships' companies, there were more everyday matters to consider and it was the first opportunity for a run ashore since the beginning of the month. Ron Lewis remembers, '...the crisp night air and a Salvation Army band playing in the city's main square. My companion and I found a "fast food" van and for just a few Kroner we purchased a very tasty stew which was called Lapscouse. It was delicious and it remains my overriding memory of Norway.'

At just before 5pm on 27 September, after the royal guests had left the ship, and after the other warships had left harbour, the *Eagle* weighed anchor and steamed down the Skagerrak to Kristiansand, where she anchored at 2pm the following afternoon for a three-day courtesy visit. Once again the *Eagle* was opened to the public and the new carrier was as popular with the Norwegians as she had been with the people of Portsmouth and Plymouth.

The *Eagle* left the Norwegian port during the afternoon of 2 October 1952 and set courses for Rosyth. Next day, at just after 9am, as a Firebrand was launched from the flight deck at the start of the day's flying exercises, it crashed into the sea but fortunately the pilot was picked up safely by HMS *Agincourt's* seaboat. That same afternoon a Firefly aircraft crashed on deck after its undercarriage collapsed while landing, and again, luckily, there were no injuries and the flight deck was quickly made serviceable once again.

After rendezvousing with the *Vanguard*, the *Eagle* anchored at Rosyth on 4 October 1952, and two days later the First Lord of the Admiralty, Mr J. P. L. Thomas, visited the ship. Most of October was spent at sea, off the north-east of Scotland, exercising with *Vanguard, Superb* and a number of destroyers of the Home Fleet. In early November, whilst at anchor off Invergordon, the C-in-C Home Fleet, Admiral Sir George Creasy, visited the ship to inspect Divisions on the flight deck, and this was followed by another week of flying and gunnery exercises.

At 4.30pm on Friday 7 November 1952, the *Eagle* anchored off Invergordon once again and the next day, with the ship's company mustered in the upper hangar, Captain Willoughby gave his farewell address before he left the carrier on promotion. At 9am on Sunday 9 November he was relieved by Captain A. N. C. Bingley RN. Following Captain Willoughby's departure at 10.15 am that day, Divisions and a Remembrance Day Service were held in the upper hangar and on the next day the *Eagle* left her anchorage to carry out further exercises off the Scottish coast. These continued until the last week in November when *Eagle* left the area to return to Devonport for Christmas. After stopping briefly off the Mull of Kintyre to catapult two wrecked Firebrands which had been damaged in the previous month, and flying off the squadrons in the Channel, *Eagle* secured alongside 5 & 6 wharves at Devonport Dockyard on the morning of 8 December 1952. It had been a busy year of operational service for the new aircraft carrier.

Chapter Three

First Commission - Coronation Review

With Christmas and New Year leave over, the children's party behind them and routine maintenance undertaken, the *Eagle* and her ship's company left Devonport on the morning of Tuesday 20 January 1953. Just over three hours later, at 11.40am, she suffered her first fatal flying accident. An Attacker aircraft, which was landing on, crashed into the sea and despite an intensive search by the seaboat, no trace could be found of the pilot, Commander H. C. Baker RN. Following this tragic start to the year there were further problems six days later when fire broke out in the bilges of Y boiler room, which necessitated the evacuation of the compartment. Fortunately there were no casualties and the smoke damage was soon repaired.

After landing on her squadrons in the Channel, the *Eagle* left UK waters for the first time and, in company with the

The *Eagle* about to make a ceremonial entry into Gibraltar Harbour in early 1953.   *(T. Heaps)*

destroyers *Battleaxe* and *Crossbow*, she steamed south for Gibraltar where she arrived on the afternoon of 3 February. After a stay of only four days she put to sea again, this time in company with the *Venus* and *Virago*, and set course for Malta, arriving in Grand Harbour during the afternoon of Friday 13 February. After firing a salute to the C-in-C Mediterranean Station, Admiral Earl Mountbatten of Burma, she was moored to 13 & 13A buoys in Bighi Bay.

Following her three-day stay *Eagle* put to sea for flying exercises with HMS *Indomitable*, and on Thursday 19 February Lord Mountbatten flew onto the ship to watch her being put through her paces and to see the jet aircraft being operated at sea. That weekend, in Grand Harbour, Lord Mountbatten inspected Divisions, and after carrying out further exercises off Malta, on the last day of February, the *Eagle* steamed west for Gibraltar. After a visit by the First Sea Lord, who arrived on board by helicopter from HMS *Vanguard*, the *Eagle's* aircraft flew off to RAF North Front and the carrier went alongside Gibraltar's South Mole on the afternoon of 5 March, this time for a six-day visit.

HMS *Eagle* left Gibraltar at 9.30am on Wednesday 11 March with the aircraft carriers *Illustrious* and *Theseus*, and that same afternoon tragedy struck once again. In the first incident an Attacker crashed into the sea, killing the pilot, Lt P. G. Ree RN, and an hour later at 4.15pm, two Sea Hornets collided in mid-air and fell into the sea 200 yards apart. From this incident there was only one survivor, and Commander C. Hart RN, together with Lieutenants J. W. Rankin RN and L. Waygood RN, were lost. Next day the *Eagle* returned to Gibraltar and on Sunday 15 March a memorial service was held for the aircrews who had been killed in the two accidents.

When the *Eagle* left Gibraltar again on the morning of Tuesday 17 March 1953, she was flying the flag of Vice-Admiral J. Hughes-Hallett, Flag Officer Heavy Squadron, and she was accompanied by the destroyer HMS *St James*. The two ships were going to pay the first formal visit by British warships for many years to the port of Vigo in north-western Spain. In view of the 'frosty' diplomatic relations which existed between Britain and Spain at that time, careful preparations had been necessary and the Foreign Office had finally 'cleared' the visit in December 1952. When the *Eagle* left Gibraltar she had on board the First Secretary to the British Embassy in Madrid, as well as a fluent Spanish-speaking officer who would act as interpreter to Vice-Admiral Hughes-Hallett. Commander T. D. Brougham RN from HMS *Eagle* travelled overland to Vigo with the Naval Attaché from the British Embassy in

A fine aerial view of the *Eagle* anchored at Spithead for the Coronation Review of June 1953, flying the flag of Vice-Admiral J. Hughes-Hallett CB. The French cruiser *Montcalm* is in the background. *(FotoFlite)*

HMS *Eagle* anchored at Spithead for the Coronation Review of the Fleet, June 1953. *(Fleet Air Arm Museum)*

Madrid, and they arrived a few days before the *Eagle* left Gibraltar. The carrier and her destroyer escort arrived in the Ria de Vigo at 8.25am on Thursday 19 March and after firing a 21-gun National Salute, at 9.05am the *Eagle* anchored some five cables from the eastern end of the port's Muelle de Transatlanticos, while the *St James* was able to berth alongside Darsena de la Large. Soon after the *Eagle* had anchored, official visitors, among them the Military Governor and the Port Captain, arrived on board and despite the fact that it happened to be a *fiesta*, all the protocol of a formal visit was observed. Although a full programme of events had been organized for FOHS and the two commanding officers, the Spanish authorities had arranged very little for the ships' companies and despite Admiral Hughes-Hallett's best endeavours, he was unable to alter the situation.

On the morning of Friday 20 March, after embarking a group of Spanish Government officials and service officers the *Eagle* and the *St James* put to sea for a 'Shop Window' flying display. Once they had arrived at the aircraft operating area off Vigo Bay, the ship's helicopter started the display with a simulated rescue of a survivor in a rubber dinghy. This was followed by the launching of six

Attackers and eight Fireflies, the former making attacks on a towed target using their 20mm cannon, while the latter carried out anti-submarine attacks using depth charges, and rocket attacks on a towed target. The final display was a joint dummy air strike on the *Eagle* by the Attackers and Fireflies, with the ship's close-range armament firing break-up shot. The aircraft were all recovered safely by 2.30pm and an hour and a half later the *Eagle* was back at her anchorage beneath the slopes of Monte del Castro.

Over the three days of the visit both the *Eagle* and the *St James* were opened to visitors and over 9,400 people went on board the carrier, while 7,500 visited the destroyer. The relatively small total in *Eagle* was not due to the fact that she was anchored offshore as plenty of boats and ferries were available, but the governing factor, according to FOHS, was that '...the construction of the ship rendered it physically impossible to accept or clear visitors at a rate of more than 800 to 1,000 per hour. In this matter she is far more difficult than any other ship which I have seen, and I view with much concern the surprise and disappointment in store for holiday crowds during the coming summer cruise who will expect to come on board, and who will be disappointed in the vast majority of cases.'

A Sea Hornet makes a dusk landing on board the *Eagle*. *(N. Curnow)*

During the four-day visit a total of 2,723 liberty men were landed from the two ships and much goodwill was fostered among the local people. However, according to FOHS's report on the visit, 'In spite of all advice a number of men could only be convinced by practical trials that the local drinks are intoxicating.'

Both the *Eagle* and the *St James* left Vigo at 8am on Monday 23 March 1953 and, although the visit was a success, Admiral Hughes-Hallett thought that, '...the same effect could have been achieved with an informal visit.'

After leaving Vigo, the following day was spent at sea with the *Eagle's* Sea Hornets carrying out flying exercises, and on the morning of Wednesday 25 March the squadrons were launched to their stations at Culdrose, Lee-on-the-Solent and Ford in Sussex. That same afternoon the ship's SAR helicopter was scrambled after an aircraft from RNAS Culdrose ditched in the sea just a few miles away from the *Eagle*, and fortunately it was able to rescue the pilot and return him to his base. Next morning, Thursday 26 March 1953, the *Eagle* entered Plymouth Sound and secured to C buoy before, later that day, steaming up-harbour to secure alongside 6 & 7 wharves of Devonport Dockyard.

Eagle's maintenance period lasted until mid-May 1953, during which time she was dry docked for over three weeks, and on Friday 15 May she was ready to put to sea once again. At 7.15am that morning the guard and band fell in on the flight deck as she prepared to sail, but at the last minute her departure was postponed and she didn't leave Devonport Dockyard until 12 hours later. Next day the *Eagle* anchored in Weymouth Bay and on Sunday 17 May the Mayor of Exeter and other civic dignitaries visited the ship to present a number of pieces of silver to mark the adoption of HMS *Eagle* by the city of Exeter. The presentation, made to Captain Bingley, took place in the lower hangar in the presence of the ship's company, and afterwards the guests were given a tour of the ship and tea in the wardroom.

Apart from putting to sea for one day to undertake degaussing trials, the *Eagle* remained at anchor in Weymouth Bay for two weeks. It was at this time that it was announced that the title of 'Fleet Air Arm' would be reinstated after a lapse of seven years, replacing the unpopular term of 'Naval Aviation' which had been used instead. The title of Fleet Air Arm had first been applied to the Royal Flying Corps squadrons which operated from and with the Navy's warships. In 1918 the Royal Naval Air Service and the Royal Flying Corps were amalgamated into the Royal Air Force, and in 1924 the Fleet Air Arm came under the joint control of the Air Ministry and the Admiralty. This was a cumbersome arrangement with the RAF being generally responsible for maintenance of the aircraft, development and administration, while the Navy provided a high proportion of aircrews and controlled actual operations. Finally, in May 1939, the Admiralty took full control of the organization, but Coastal

'Exercise Mariner', which took place in the Denmark Strait during late September and early October 1953, was marked by severe weather. In this view parked Fireflies get a drenching. *(N. Curnow)*

Command remained with the RAF and has done ever since. After the war the Admiralty decided to introduce the title of Naval Aviation because it was felt that the original name tended to divide naval aviators from sea officers. However, despite the change, the name Fleet Air Arm continued to be used and, finally, in May 1953 this fact was recognized and it was officially reintroduced.

The latter half of May was a busy period for the ship's company of HMS *Eagle* as the coronation of Queen Elizabeth II had been set for 2 June, and 13 days later Her Majesty would review the fleet at Spithead. It was the first Fleet Review since the Coronation Review of May 1937 and there had been many changes to the make-up of the Navy in the intervening 16 years. Gone were the great battleships such as *Queen Elizabeth*, *Ramillies*, *Revenge*, *Rodney* and *Nelson*. Even the recent King George V class had disappeared from the operational scene and, in fact, in 1953 the Royal Navy had only one of the great leviathans left with the fleet, HMS *Vanguard*, a beautiful ship armed with eight 15-inch guns,* and although she was flying the

flag of the C-in-C Home Fleet, Admiral Sir George Creasy, there is no doubt that during this review she would be eclipsed by the eight aircraft carriers present. Of these new capital ships the pride of place would go to the *Eagle*, as the newest and the largest of the warships on show.

During the last few days of May, as a holiday atmosphere became apparent throughout the country, *Eagle*'s street lining party rehearsed their Coronation Day duties at Portland's Camber Jetty and the ship itself was thrown open to visitors, proving once again to be very popular with the public. Finally, on the afternoon of Friday 29 May 1953, the *Eagle* weighed anchor to steam up Channel for an official visit to Brighton. Next day, at 7.15am, she anchored three miles south-south-west of the town, only to become embroiled in the civic jealousies which exist between Brighton and its smaller neighbour, Hove. No sooner had the carrier anchored, than protests were made to the effect that, although the *Eagle*'s visit was officially to Brighton, she was actually anchored off Hove. Fortunately the navigating officer was able to answer the

* Ironically these guns had been fitted in the light battlecruisers *Courageous* and *Glorious* in 1916, but they were removed when the two ships were converted to aircraft carriers in the early 1920s.

Eagle's quarterdeck gets a wash down during 'Mariner'.

(N. Curnow)

complaints by assuring everyone concerned that, although from some angles the ship appeared to be lying off Hove, he had actually chosen the *Eagle's* anchorage very carefully and she was, in fact, in a position about half a mile inside the western boundary of Brighton in seven and a half fathoms of water at high tide. That same afternoon, as municipal etiquette demanded, the Mayor of Brighton went to call on Admiral Hughes-Hallett. The plan was that the Mayor would board the ship's helicopter on the lawns of the Royal Pavilion, but it was unable to land in the designated area and so the pilot flew along the seafront, followed by the Mayor's car and escort, and finally landed on Brunswick Lawns. Unfortunately the pilot had, unknowingly, come down inside the borough of Hove and the Mayor of Brighton refused to travel the few hundred yards necessary to reach the helicopter declaring that, 'It would not be etiquette to enter another borough wearing the mayoral chain. In any case, the citizens of Brighton would not expect me to start this historic journey from another town.'

Faced with this impasse it was suggested that the helicopter fly to the grounds of Roedean School where the Mayor could embark within his borough boundaries, and this being acceptable the pilot took off and flew low over the seafront, again with the mayoral car and escort following behind. Fortunately this arrangement was successful and the Mayor of Brighton was able to make his official call on Admiral Hughes-Hallett, while the helicopter pilot was left to ponder the petty jealousies which had turned a simple operation into something of a farce.

Fortunately the remainder of the nine-day visit went without a hitch. By 8am on Tuesday 2 June 1953 the ship was dressed overall for the coronation of Her Majesty Queen Elizabeth II, and two and a half hours later *Eagle's* 21-gun salute reverberated along the seafronts of both Brighton and Hove. At 5pm the order was given to 'Splice the Main Brace' and over the following three days the ship was opened to visitors each afternoon.

The *Eagle* finally weighed anchor and left Brighton at 5pm on Monday 8 June 1953, to make an overnight passage to Spithead, and at 9.45am the next day she took her place in F line of the Review Fleet, between HMS *Vanguard* and HMS *Indomitable.* Throughout the next day the warships continued to assemble, including the US Navy's heavy cruiser USS *Baltimore* (Vice-Admiral J. Wright USN) and the Soviet cruiser *Sverdlov* (Captain O. I. Rudauov). By Friday 12 June the assembly of the Spithead Review Fleet was complete, and on the evening of Sunday 14 June Her Majesty The Queen arrived by car at South Railway Jetty in Portsmouth Harbour, to be received by the Lord Mayor of Portsmouth and the C-in-C Portsmouth, before embarking in HMS *Surprise* where the Royal Standard was broken and the ships of the Review Fleet dressed overall.

HMS *Surprise*, which was to serve as the Royal Yacht for the Review, had actually been completed as the Loch-class frigate HMS *Loch Carron*, but she was renamed *Surprise* in 1945 and fitted with extra accommodation to serve as the C-in-C's yacht on the Mediterranean Station. For the Review her twin 4-inch gun mounting was removed in order to provide a viewing platform for the Queen.

Meanwhile, by 8am on Monday 15 June 1953 the Review Fleet had once again dressed overall and soon afterwards the first guests arrived on board the *Eagle*, including 700 boys from the training establishments HMS *Ganges* and HMS *St Vincent*. Finally, at 2.30pm, the order to clear lower deck was given and the *Eagle's* ship's company fell in on the flight deck. At 3pm HMS *Surprise*, preceded by the Trinity House vessel *Patricia* and escorted by HMS *Redpole,* left South Railway Jetty for Spithead. At 3.15pm, on the approach of the *Surprise*, the fleet fired a royal salute of 21 guns. However, as the spectacle in Spithead unfolded, there was a different drama on board the *Eagle* when one of the guests, Mrs W. G. S. McCracken, safely gave birth to a

Although the *Eagle* pitched and rolled heavily during the exercise 'Mariner' Norman Curnow recalls: '...whenever we felt queasy we just looked over at RFA *Olna*...

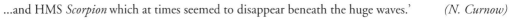

...and HMS *Scorpion* which at times seemed to disappear beneath the huge waves.'   (*N. Curnow*)

The US Navy's battleship *Iowa* steams past the *Eagle* shortly after the end of 'Exercise Mariner'. Fireflies and a Sea Hornet are parked on the carrier's deck.   *(N. Curnow)*

daughter, who was appropriately named Elizabeth. Shortly afterwards, at 3.30pm, the *Patricia* passed ahead of the *Eagle*, followed five minutes later by the Royal Yacht. The cheers of the ship's company, augmented by the 700 boy seamen, could be heard all round the Solent. Following the Royal Yacht were four escorting frigates, all carrying official guests, and following behind them were three liners, *Orcades*, *Pretoria Castle* and *Strathnaver*. At the end of the line were the two Isle of Wight ferries *Brading* and *Southsea*, which were carrying Admiralty guests.

The Review was concluded at 5.15pm when HMS *Surprise* anchored at the head of E line and the fly-past of the Fleet Air Arm Squadrons, including the *Eagle's* aircraft, began. Amongst the aircraft flying over Spithead that day were the Avengers of 849 Squadron, led by their commanding officer Lt-Cdr J. D. Treacher RN who, 15 years later, would command the *Eagle* herself.

That evening the celebrations continued with a firework display, and as darkness fell the fleet at Spithead was bathed in light as all the ships switched on their illuminations. Next morning, as HMS *Surprise* left the Review lines, the fleet fired another royal salute, then during the afternoon all the remaining vessels left the area to return to their

various stations. It had been a successful occasion which would be remembered vividly by all those who took part.

The *Eagle* weighed anchor at just before 4pm that day, and as she steamed down Channel to Devonport the Attackers of 800 and 803 Squadrons were landed on. After just a few hours at C buoy in Plymouth Sound the carrier set course for Rosyth by way of the Irish Sea and en route she landed on the Fireflies of 812 Squadron and the Sea Hornets of 809 Squadron. There then followed 25 days of exercises off the north-east coast of Scotland in company with HMS *Swiftsure* and the 4th Destroyer Squadron. It was during these exercises, early on the morning of Thursday 9 July 1953, that a fatal accident took place on the *Eagle's* flight deck which is recalled here by Terry Heaps, an aircraft handler: 'We were night flying at the time and the accident happened in the early hours of the morning at around 4am when we were ranging Sea Hornets for take-off, and the flight deck was parked herringbone range. The Sea Hornet was a particularly dangerous aircraft as the propellers were positioned very close to the wheels and we literally had to lie on the chocks whilst the aircraft revved up and warmed through their engines. This particular morning Andrew "Paddy" Smith, a cheerful young lad

In October 1953 the *Eagle* carried out deck landing trials with Westland Wyvern aircraft. *(Fleet Air Arm Museum)*

from Belfast, must have been tired and not concentrating for when he got the order, "away chocks", he ran straight into the Hornet's propeller and was decapitated.'

That evening the *Eagle* anchored in the Moray Firth and the following day, at the conclusion of flying operations, the body of Naval Airman Andrew Smith was committed to the deep.

On Thursday 16 July, with the exercises completed, the *Eagle* left the Invergordon area and steamed via the Pentland Firth to the Lancashire coast where she anchored five miles west of the seaside resort of Blackpool. For the Mayor and his guests there was a long, and choppy, boat ride out to the official reception on board, and those members of the ship's company who wished to sample the resort's 'Golden Mile' had to make a similar journey in the opposite direction. After a stay of just over 30 hours the *Eagle* weighed anchor and made the short voyage north to Fleetwood where she anchored some three miles north-west of the town. This time the visit lasted for three days, although at one time, with heavy rain and poor visibility, it appeared that the ship's stay would have to be cut short. Fortunately this was not necessary and at 7.30am on Wednesday 22 July, on schedule, the *Eagle* weighed anchor

and set course for Devonport, arriving alongside 6 & 7 wharves the following afternoon.

It was during the *Eagle's* stay in Devonport that a number of minor, but disturbing, acts of sabotage took place on board which gained media publicity out of proportion to the damage caused. Soon after her arrival in Devonport a number of glass water gauges were found to have been deliberately broken and it was clear that the damage was being caused by one or two individuals who, for personal reasons, had decided to behave unpleasantly. As soon as it was realized that the damage was deliberate, all CPOs, POs and Leading Hands were addressed by the Captain and asked to keep extra vigilance, and fortunately it was not long before two Stoker Mechanics were arrested and charged with malicious damage. Investigations eventually revealed that the two individuals concerned had damaged 14 telephones, 29 pressure gauges, the boiler room telegraph and the glass faces of four fan speed indicators. Both men were sentenced to three years' imprisonment and dismissed from the Service. Unfortunately the incidents made headlines in the national Press and it was an illustration of how irresponsible behaviour by one or two people can tarnish the good reputation of a ship's company earned by the hard work and great effort of the majority.

Despite the problems there were some amusing incidents during this period, one of which is recalled by Terry Heaps: 'Soon after we returned home in July 1953 my mate, Cameron Hamilton, and I were loaned out to the seamen branch in order to help with painting ship whilst we were in harbour and we soon got used to working with the side party, painting the hull of the ship from rope and steel nets. It made a nice change to work with the "fishheads". We always took it in turns to go down in the bosun's chair to chip the paintwork which had to be replaced. On this particular day we were painting sections of the ship's side just beneath the flight deck and it was "Cammie's" turn in the bosun's chair, with me lowering him from the flight deck to a spot about 15 feet below. We were on the starboard side just forward of the island and "Cammie" got in the chair as usual and I, with two turns of the rope around a large cleat, started to lower him. I shouted to him to call me when he reached his "spot" and he shouted back, "okay". Well, at that moment it started to rain and I took shelter under a bofors gun confident that I would still be able to hear him when he called to me. Anyway, I lowered , and lowered, and lowered the chair and I heard no call from "Cammie". Suddenly I realized that I had let out a great deal of rope which worried me somewhat and I decided to look over the side to see if "Cammie" was all right. There he was thrashing about in the water of Devonport Dockyard with half of the ship's company on the weather decks laughing their heads off. It was quite hilarious at the time and the whole ship knew about it. Whenever I walked into the cafeteria a loud cheer would go up with shouts of, "That's the "B" that drops you in it." The story was even mentioned on Daily Orders as an example of how you should *not* lower a bosun's chair. Needless to say, after that I was on the chair every time.'

During the Navy Days of early August that year the *Eagle* was opened to visitors over three days and nearly 20,000 people went on board. By Monday 31 August 1953 the *Eagle* was preparing for sea once again and that afternoon the ground parties of 800 and 803 (Attacker) Squadrons, 809 (Sea Hornet) Squadron, 814 and 825 (Firefly) Squadrons and 849 Skyraider Squadron, joined the ship. Next morning at just after 11am, and once again wearing the flag of FOHS, Vice-Admiral J. S. Hughes-Hallett, the *Eagle* left Devonport Dockyard and put to sea, bound for northern waters and the NATO exercise 'Mariner'. On Wednesday 2 September, as she steamed north through the Irish Sea, the squadrons were safely landed on and four days later she rendezvoused with HMS *Vanguard* and other units of the Home Fleet off the northeast coast of Scotland. 'Exercise Mariner' started on Tuesday 22 September in the Denmark Strait and with the

severe weather at the time flying was only possible on three of the 11 days that the exercise lasted. Norman Curnow, who was an Aircraft Artificer with 809 Squadron recalls, '...our role in "Exercise Mariner" which, for 11 days found us in the Denmark Strait and in such severe weather that our aircraft were "grounded". The *Eagle* pitched and rolled heavily but, for consolation, whenever we felt a bit queasy, we just looked over at RFA *Olna* and the destroyer *Scorpion*, which at times seemed to disappear beneath the huge waves. During the exercise our meals seemed to consist wholly of stew, or stew with pastry, and this prompted one US Navy CPO who was with us at the time to comment, "Gee, you Limeys sure eat to live".'

'Exercise Mariner' ended on the morning of Saturday 3 October 1953, when the *Eagle* anchored off Greenock for the weekend before steaming round the Pentland Firth to Lossiemouth for the C-in-C Home Fleet's inspection. During the voyage one of the helicopters ditched alongside the planeguard destroyer, HMS *Duchess*. Although the crew member, Leading Telegraphist Snell, was injured he did manage to escape from the wrecked aircraft, but despite an intensive search there was no trace of the pilot, Lt P. S. Bough RN. After transferring the ship's surgeon to the *Duchess*, the destroyer was detached to Invergordon to land the casualty and the *Eagle* flew off her squadrons before she too secured to the flagship buoy at Invergordon. The C-in-C's inspection of the ship lasted for most of Thursday 15 October, starting with Divisions on the flight deck.

On 20 October 1953, following the successful conclusion of the C-in-C's inspection, the *Eagle* left Invergordon to return to the Channel, and during that morning she recovered the aircraft which had been sent to Lossiemouth. Before the end of the month three terrible accidents took place, two of them proving to be fatal and one causing very serious injuries. The first of these happened when the *Eagle's* own aircraft were carrying out dummy attacks on the ship and the gun crews were closed up and firing break-up shot. Unfortunately one of the stops which prevent one gun firing towards another was not functioning, and Boy First Class M. V. Aldridge was badly injured in the face and chest when particles of shot fired by an adjoining gun hit him. Despite prompt attention the ship's surgeon was unable to save his eyesight and he was permanently blinded.

The second accident happened on the flight deck on the morning of Thursday 22 October 1953, just before flying operations started for the day, and it is recalled by Terry Heaps who was a member of the flight deck fire crew that morning: 'The flight deck was very busy with about 36 aircraft on deck, arranged in a herringbone and all at different stages of warming up. In the bright morning sunlight the propellers were often hard to see and one's wits had to be razor sharp at all times. I remember Leading Airman Wainwright was running to load two smoke floats onto a Sea Fury and, unfortunately, he must have had a lapse of concentration for he ran straight into an "invisible" propeller and was literally ripped to pieces.' The following day Leading Airman A. A. Wainwright's body was committed to the deep in a position Lat 50° - 12'N/Long 05° - 54'W, and the *Eagle* anchored at Spithead for the weekend. On Monday 26 October 1953 the *Eagle* weighed anchor once again and steamed into the exercise area south of the Isle of Wight where flying operations were resumed.

It was on Thursday 29 October that the third accident occurred, when *Eagle* was carrying out catapult and deck landing trials with Wyvern aircraft. Norman Curnow remembers the incident: 'Whilst we were carrying out deck landing trials off the Isle of Wight a Wyvern "nosed down" as it arrested, and the contra-rotating propellers touched the flight deck and shattered with a shrapnel effect. Unfortunately an aircraft handler, Petty Officer J. A. Kirby, was hit by fragments of the propellers and he was killed.' On the morning of Friday 30 October 1953, for the second time in seven days, a funeral service was held and the body of Petty Officer J. A. Kirby was committed to the deep in a position which was very close to where Leading Airman Wainwright had also been buried at sea.

After spending the weekend anchored in Weymouth Bay, on the morning of Monday 2 November the *Eagle*, with the cruiser *Apollo*, put to sea once again, this time to carry out trials with Sea Venom aircraft which included night landing exercises. By the morning of Thursday 12 November these trials had been completed and the Sea Venoms were flown off to Boscombe Down while the *Eagle* anchored at Spithead for a long weekend before setting sail for her second visit to Vigo. It was at just before 9am on Tuesday 17 November, whilst she was en route to northwest Spain, that another tragic fatal accident took place. Again it is recalled by Terry Heaps: 'It involved Naval Airman Francis "Geordie" Routledge, who was a catapult officer's assistant. It was his job to carry the different coloured flags and the clipboard for the lieutenant who actually fired the aircraft off the catapults, and on this occasion a Skyraider was being loaded onto a catapult. Unfortunately, as the aircraft swung round, the air blast caught "Geordie" and blew him over the ship's side. Sadly, as he fell, his head struck one of the 4·5-inch gun barrels and if it hadn't been for that he would probably have survived.' In fact it took only 15 minutes for the seaboat to reach the unfortunate man, but he was already dead, and the following afternoon yet another funeral was held at sea as the body of Naval Airman F. A. Routledge was committed to the deep in a position Lat 48° - 55'N/Long 07° - 05'W.

During the morning of Saturday 21 November 1953 the *Eagle* and the *Apollo* arrived in Vigo Bay for a four-day visit to the port, and following this the *Eagle* carried out a three-day trial of the prototype Bristol 173, tandem rotored, twin-engined helicopter. This 30-seat utility helicopter had first flown in January 1952, but it was never developed beyond the experimental stage.

In the early afternoon of Tuesday 1 December 1953 the *Eagle* steamed through Plymouth Sound and secured alongside 5 & 6 wharves of Devonport Dockyard and the ship's company prepared for their Christmas and New Year leave. It had been a busy year which had been marred by a series of unfortunate accidents.

On 21 November 1953 the *Eagle* visited Vigo in north-west Spain. Here she makes her entry into Vigo Bay. From the stern looking forward there are six Skyraiders, six Sea Hornets, six Fireflies, 12 Attackers and the captain's launch ranged on deck.

(N. Curnow & Fleet Air Arm Museum)

Chapter Four

First Commission - Mediterranean Fleet

Seven days after going alongside at Devonport, Vice-Admiral J. Hughes-Hallett struck his flag and left the *Eagle* for an appointment in the Admiralty, while Rear-Admiral R. A. Couchman assumed the duties of FOHS and hoisted his flag in the carrier.

Ten days later, on 18 December, there was another case of malicious damage on board when 11 pressure gauges in one of the engine rooms were found to have been damaged. Fortunately the culprit, a Stoker Mechanic, was quickly apprehended and sentenced to 15 months' detention. Sadly, the publicity that this untoward incident attracted was out of all proportion and, once again, it reflected badly on all the hard work which had been put in by the rest of the ship's company.

Later that same month, on Tuesday 29 December, Rear-Admiral A.N.C. Bingley left the ship on promotion and the *Eagle's* new commanding officer, Captain D.E. Holland-Martin DSO DSC RN, assumed command. Four weeks later, on 26 January 1954, with all the seasonal leave having been taken, the *Eagle* slipped her berth in Devonport and, in company with the cruiser *Apollo*, she set course for Spithead. While she was steaming east in the Channel the aircraft were recovered and the 7,000th deck landing was made by a US Navy pilot in an Avenger. At Spithead the personnel of 806 Squadron, the first unit to operate Sea Hawk aircraft, were embarked and after spending the weekend at Spithead the *Eagle* left the area on Monday 1 February and safely recovered the first Sea Hawks. Norman Curnow remembers the occasion: 'I can remember the "awed" voice from Flyco announcing, "The next aircraft to land is being flown by an RAF officer and this is his first deck landing." Later in the *Eagle's* career young pilots would land Sea Vixens and Buccaneers with even less flying hours in.'

With the embarkation of 806 Squadron the *Eagle* had over 60 aircraft in her hangars which included Attackers, Avengers, Sea Hornets, Skyraiders and Dragonfly helicopters in addition to the Sea Hawks. However, already it was clear that the new carrier was becoming outdated as a result of the rapid developments in naval aviation and arrangements were being made in the Admiralty to design a new angled flight deck which would be installed during her next refit.

After spending six days exercising in the Channel, on Monday 8 February both the *Eagle* and the *Apollo* left home waters for the Mediterranean and two days later, in the Bay of Biscay, a Sea Hornet was lost overboard. Norman Curnow recalls the incident: 'Whilst crossing the Bay of Biscay through a heavy sea, one of our Sea Hornets, whose brakes were unserviceable, was being struck down.

In January 1954 the *Eagle* operated Sea Hawks for the first time. Here a Hawk of 806 Squadron lands on. In the background is HMS *Apollo* and a Dragonfly helicopter.
(Fleet Air Arm Museum)

The *Eagle* alongside at the French naval base of Mers-el-Kebir in Algeria.

(N. Curnow)

Another view of the *Eagle* at Mers-el-Kebir. French warships can be seen in the background while in the foreground is part of the RFA *Black Ranger*, which was accompanying the *Eagle*. (N. Curnow)

Unfortunately the aircraft jumped the chocks and as it ran loose across the flight deck it hit an Attacker then, as the ship rolled heavily to port, it trundled off in the opposite direction and fell overboard. At the time we were not at flying stations and as most of the aircraft were fully serviceable the majority of the maintenance crews were down below in their mess decks. When "Clear lower deck - 809 Squadron - muster in the lower hangar" was piped, most of them thought that they were going to have to clean the aircraft so there was no rush to get there. Needless to say they weren't very popular when they all finally arrived for a headcount, as it wasn't known if there had been anyone in the cockpit of the Hornet when it went overboard. Fortunately the aircraft had been empty which wasn't always the case, even when there were no brakes to operate.'

The last two weeks of February 1954 were spent exercising in the Straits of Gibraltar with the *Scorpion* and the *Apollo*, with weekends alongside at Gibraltar. It was on 17 February, during these exercises, that 806 Squadron lost its first Sea Hawk, but fortunately the pilot bailed out safely and was picked up by the SAR helicopter. Five days later, at 3.20pm on Monday 22 February, an Attacker, which was launched from the port catapult, turned over and dived into the sea. Despite the fact that the SAR helicopter was scrambled immediately and the seaboat was launched, there was no sign of the aircraft or its pilot, Lt James F. Nash RN. Selwyn Maund, who was a Boy

Seaman at the time, remembers this tragic accident clearly: 'I was off duty at the time and I had gone up to the goofing deck on the island during the afternoon to watch the flying exercises. An Attacker was fired off one of the catapults on what should have been just another routine flight, but it just ditched into the sea off the port side. I can still remember the feeling of utter helplessness as I watched the sinking aircraft float by and saw the pilot struggling to open his canopy, but with the ship still steaming at speed he was left behind very quickly and could not be rescued. It was yet another death on board.'

Next day, as the *Eagle* set course for Mers-el-Kebir in what was then French Algeria, a memorial service was held for Lt Nash. The visit to the French naval base was the first since the end of World War II and Norman Curnow describes the atmosphere on board: 'Our visit to the French naval base of Mers-el-Kebir in Algeria was notable

HMS *Eagle* in the Mediterranean in company with HMS *Apollo*. The carrier has Attackers, Fireflies and Skyraiders ranged on the flight deck.

(Fleet Air Arm Museum)

as we were the first RN ship to call there following the end of the Second World War. There was some apprehension on board as to how we would be received, in view of "Operation Catapult" where, in July 1940, the Royal Navy had sunk or disabled most of the French Fleet at the port. However, our fears were groundless for, when the ship was opened to the public, we were besieged by a very enthusiastic and friendly local population. We even had problems getting away from the port with a strong wind holding the *Eagle* firmly against the jetty.'

The *Eagle* had secured alongside the jetty in the naval base at Mers-el-Kebir at just before 9am on Friday 26 February 1954, and during her four-day stay she was opened to visitors each afternoon. When the time came for sailing, as Norman Curnow recalled, high winds were blowing across the harbour which delayed her departure by an hour, but she finally left during the morning of Tuesday

2 March and returned to Gibraltar. The following week *Eagle* was at sea again and taking part in joint exercises with HMS *Barrosa* and the Dutch aircraft carrier HMNS *Karel Doorman**. Following a long weekend alongside in Gibraltar, the *Eagle* put to sea once again, this time for 'Exercise Toughline' with the Daring-class destroyers *Decoy, Duchess* and *Diamond* and the older destroyers *Agincourt, Crossbow, Scorpion* and *Corunna*, as well as the carriers *Implacable* and *Indefatigable*. During these exercises the Soviet ship *Kuban* kept a close eye on proceedings and, in turn, the *Eagle's* helicopter took a series of photographs of the intruder.

At the end of this exercise the *Eagle* returned to Gibraltar where, as Norman Curnow remembers, the following incident occurred: 'As we manoeuvred to our berth alongside the South Mole, between the *Implacable* and the *Vanguard,* which was forward of us, our stern collided with the

---

* Ex-HMS *Venerable,* sold to the Royal Netherlands Navy in April 1948. In October 1968 she was sold to Argentina and renamed *Vienticino De Mayo.* During the Falklands War in 1982 she did not venture out of harbour.

On Monday 29 March 1954 an Attacker made a very skilful landing after its undercarriage failed. Fortunately the pilot was not injured.

(*S. Maund*)

The *Eagle* alongside Gibraltar's South Mole on 19 March 1954. She is between the battleship HMS *Vanguard* and the aircraft carrier HMS *Implacable*.

(*N. Curnow*)

"Implac's" bow. Shortly after this a signal was received saying, "Thank you. We wanted to get in early with an angled deck." With our Sea Hornet aircraft having flown back to the UK, we ground crews embarked in the *Implacable* for the voyage home and 809 Squadron re-formed at RNAS Yeovilton with Sea Venoms replacing the Hornets.' After ten days alongside at Gibraltar, on Monday 29 March *Eagle* left for more flying exercises and for an official visit to Toulon. During the flying operations that day an Attacker made a very skilful landing when its undercarriage failed. Fortunately the pilot was uninjured, but the damaged aircraft was catapulted into the sea that afternoon.

The *Eagle* arrived alongside at Toulon on Saturday 3 April and during the visit the C-in-C Mediterranean Fleet, Admiral Lord Mountbatten, accompanied by Lady Mountbatten, toured the ship. The visit to the French port ended on Tuesday 6 April when the *Eagle* left for Naples. During the passage, manoeuvres were rehearsed for *Eagle's* rendezvous with the new Royal Yacht *Britannia* when she arrived in Malta from Tobruk at the end of the Queen's Commonwealth tour.

At 7.30am on Friday 9 April 1954 the *Eagle* was in the Tyrrhenian Sea, east of Tavolara Island, Sardinia, when she received an urgent signal from the C-in-C Mediterranean: 'Proceed to investigate crash of Comet IV airliner in position Lat 39° - 52'N/Long 14° - 16'E.' As soon as he read the signal Captain Holland-Martin altered course and ordered full speed from all four engine rooms in order to reach the disaster scene as quickly as possible.

The BOAC Comet IV, G-ALYY, had left London for Johannesburg at 3pm on Wednesday 7 April 1954, piloted by Captain Roy Millichap. It had landed safely in Rome, but was then delayed at the city's airport for 24 hours while a fuel gauge was repaired. Then with a new crew of six under Captain W. K. Mostert, and 14 passengers, the aircraft finally took off from Rome at 6.25pm on Thursday 8 April and it was due in Cairo at 9.20pm the same evening. Thirty-two minutes after taking off the pilot reported: 'Over Naples, still climbing' - then nothing more was heard. When the aircraft failed to arrive at Cairo it was posted as 'overdue', but in the early hours of 9 April it was listed as 'missing' and a full-scale air-sea search was initiated.

Soon after receiving the signal *Eagle's* Avengers were launched to carry out a search and at 11.42 that morning one of the aircraft reported wreckage floating in a position Lat 39° - 39'N/Long 14° - 43'E, which was about 30 miles north of Stromboli. By 6pm that evening the *Eagle* had arrived at the scene and Selwyn Maund recalls what he saw: 'I was closed up on the bridge during the last dogwatch, and I was the lookout on the starboard side. It was just after 7pm when I sighted the first wreckage which consisted of passenger seats, suitcases, ladies' handbags and holdalls floating in the water. There was also one body. I immediately reported my sightings to the Officer of the Watch, and the ship was stopped and the seaboat was lowered.' By 8pm that evening the seaboat had recovered two bodies, the pilot's log, a mailbag and wreckage, and during the following two hours the pinnace recovered a further three bodies, another mailbag and more wreckage. By now though darkness had fallen so the search was called off for the night and it was resumed at 5am the next morning, Saturday 10 April. However, soon after the operation recommenced, it became clear that nothing else of significance would be found, and at 7am it was finally called off. The *Eagle* then set course for Naples where she arrived at 3.30pm. Later that afternoon, after bodies and wreckage had been disembarked, Captain Holland-Martin met representatives of BOAC to discuss the disaster and the *Eagle's* role in the search and rescue mission.

After three days in Naples the *Eagle*, together with other units of the Mediterranean Fleet, left the port for Malta and that is where the aircraft carrier was on Thursday 22 April 1954 when *Britannia*, fresh from the builder's yard on the River Clyde, arrived in Grand Harbour.

The Queen and the Duke of Edinburgh had started their Commonwealth tour by air, and then joined the chartered passenger liner *Gothic* on 21 November 1953 in Jamaica. From there the *Gothic*, which had been converted to a Royal Yacht for the tour, sailed via Panama to Fiji, Tonga, New Zealand, Australia, Ceylon (Sri Lanka), and then to Aden where the royal party disembarked before flying on to Entebbe in Uganda. From there they would fly to Tobruk in Libya where, on 30 April, they would embark in the *Britannia* which had steamed from Malta to meet them.

On board the *Britannia* for the voyage from the UK were Prince Charles and Princess Anne who were travelling out to meet their parents, and during their stay in Malta, before sailing to Tobruk, Captain Holland-Martin entertained them on board the *Eagle* during the morning of Sunday 25 April. Six days later, on Saturday 1 May, *Eagle*, together with other ships of the Mediterranean Fleet including the cruisers *Bermuda*, *Glasgow* and *Gambia*, put to sea in order to practise manoeuvres before meeting the Royal Yacht on the following day.

The morning of Sunday 2 May dawned bright and sunny, and although there was a strong wind blowing there was no danger of it affecting the ceremonial steam-past by the ships of the fleet. After the BBC commentator Richard Dimbleby had been flown to HMS *Glasgow*, the hands fell in to man the flight deck at 10.30am. Half an hour later the 15 ships of the Mediterranean Fleet led by the *Glasgow*, which was flying the flag of Admiral Lord Mountbatten, met the *Britannia* and her close escort of four frigates to complete the passage back to Malta with them. As they bore down in line at 25 knots on either side of the Royal Yacht they all fired a coordinated 21-gun salute, and then as they passed within half a cable of the *Britannia*, officers and ratings cheered ship. After the ships had taken up stations around the Royal Yacht, aircraft from the *Eagle*

Above: Manoeuvres with HMS *Apollo* in the Mediterranean during spring 1954. *(N. Curnow)*

With Mount Vesuvius in the background, the *Eagle* approaches Naples on the afternoon of Saturday 10 April 1954.

(Fleet Air Arm Museum)

flew past at intervals with the helicopters of 845 Squadron following them, before landing on board the carrier. Next morning *Britannia*, followed by the rest of the fleet, entered Malta's magnificent Grand Harbour to a very enthusiastic welcome and the *Eagle* berthed at No 13 buoy in Bighi Bay, beneath the imposing Naval Hospital.

The following day, at 10.30am, the *Eagle's* ship's company fell in on the flight deck and, despite the fact that a strong north-westerly wind was blowing, the Queen and Duke of Edinburgh embarked and Her Majesty took the salute at a march past, after which Captain Holland-Martin conducted his royal guests on a tour of the upper hangar, where they inspected the aircraft and a display of safety equipment. After an hour on board the royal visitors disembarked to transfer to HMS *Glasgow* where they were received by Admiral Lord Mountbatten.

At 4.30pm on Friday 7 May *Britannia*, with the Queen and Duke of Edinburgh on board and accompanied by HMS *Glasgow*, left harbour at the start of the voyage home. Once again the fleet fired a coordinated 21-gun royal salute and officers and men cheered ship as the Royal Yacht left harbour. Next day, by command of Her Majesty, the order to the Mediterranean Fleet was, 'Splice the Main Brace!'.

HMS *Eagle* left Grand Harbour for Gibraltar on Tuesday 18 May 1954 and en route she carried out rehearsals for a series of 'Shop Window' flying displays which were to be carried out later that month and in early June. At Gibraltar *Eagle* anchored offshore for only five hours and after embarking 91 Army personnel for passage to the UK she weighed anchor and set course for home. She arrived at Spithead on the morning of Wednesday 26 May and the following day she put to sea for flying operations. The displays started on the last day of May and continued for five days, during which time the carrier played host to a wide range of guests from the Ministry of Defence, Members of Parliament and visitors from the Joint Services Staff College, as well as boys under training at HMS *St Vincent* in Gosport. Each morning a group of visitors would be ferried out to the ship in Sandown Bay and then she would weigh anchor and steam into the Channel where the manoeuvres were carried out. In the afternoon the *Eagle* returned to her anchorage where the guests disembarked into MFVs to return to shore. On the evening of Friday 4 June, after disembarking visitors from the Army Staff College, the *Eagle* weighed anchor and set course for Plymouth and next morning she berthed alongside 5 & 6 wharves of Devonport Dockyard.

For the remainder of the month the ship's company were employed destoring and de-ammunitioning ship and on Monday 21 June the flag of FOHS, Rear-Admiral Couchman, was struck. Seven days later, on Monday 28 June 1954, the carrier was delivered into dockyard hands for an eight-month refit. The *Eagle's* first commission, which had lasted for almost three years, had now been completed.

On Sunday 25 April 1954, Captain Holland-Martin invited Prince Charles and Princess Anne on board the *Eagle*. They were in Malta to await the arrival of their parents at the end of their Commonwealth Tour. *(Lady D. E. Holland-Martin)*

On Sunday 2 May 1954, with the ship's company manning the flight deck and the Whirlwind helicopters of 845 Squadron ranged on deck, the *Eagle* prepares to steam past the Royal Yacht. *(Lady D. E. Holland-Martin)*

The Queen takes the salute as the *Eagle* steams past the Royal Yacht *Britannia* at 11.15am on 2 May 1954.

(Lady D. E. Holland-Martin)

An aerial view of the *Eagle* as she steams past the Royal Yacht on a blustery, but fine, day.

(Lady D. E. Holland-Martin)

The *Eagle* arrives in Grand Harbour on the morning of Monday 3 May 1954. *(M. Cassar)*

Captain Holland-Martin welcomes the Queen on board the *Eagle* on the morning of Wednesday 5 May 1954 and...

...Her Majesty takes the salute as the ship's company march past on the flight deck. *(Lady D. E. Holland-Martin)*

Chapter Five

Second Commission - The First Year

During the *Eagle's* first long refit the biggest single task was to fit the carrier with an interim 5¹/₂° angled flight deck, which entailed extending the deck to the port side with the port forward 4.5-inch gun mountings forming part of the deck support. However, the refit came too early for the ship to be fitted with steam catapults which, once again, was an indication of the rapid developments which were taking place in naval aviation during the 1950s.

On 2 September 1954 a dockyard employee was killed in an explosion in an empty aviation fuel tank on board the *Eagle*, and in the following month a series of minor fires on board indicated the presence of another saboteur. The first two on 10 October 1954 were in 5P2 Stoker Mechanics' mess deck and in the after engine room, and they were clearly started deliberately. It was after a third fire, which had been started with a bale of rags close to the Damage Control HQ on 7 Deck, that precautions were taken to reduce the numbers of both dockyard workmen and members of the ship's company on board the ship after working hours, and extra security patrols were provided. However, despite these measures, three more fires were started on different days and, fortunately, because of the extra security, all of them were extinguished before any serious damage was caused. With the ship high and dry in No 10 dry dock, more security patrols were provided, including plain clothes officers from the Admiralty Constabulary. Finally the vigilance paid off for, at 11.15pm on 31 October 1954, Commissioned Writer H. F. Kendrick, who was the duty security officer, saw a shadowy figure entering the ship by the roped-off, starboard forward gangway. He immediately raised the alarm and a search was started at the forward end of the ship. Within minutes a man was spotted by two CID officers, a chase ensued and he was quickly arrested. Immediately afterwards another fire was found in the Petty Officers' dining hall but, fortunately, it was quickly extinguished. Subsequently a Stoker Mechanic was convicted of Malicious Damage, sentenced to 60 days' detention and dismissed the Service.

On 18 January 1955, with the refit coming to an end, the *Eagle's* new commanding officer, Captain E. D. G. Lewin CBE DSO DSC RN, joined the ship. Captain Lewin had served as a cadet in HMS *Royal Oak* and in 1935 he had specialized in flying. During the Second World War he had served in HMS *Ajax* during the River Plate action and he had commanded 808 Squadron in HMS *Ark Royal*. After the war he had commanded the

Colossus-class light fleet carrier HMS *Glory* during operations off Korea, and off Malaya during the campaign against the Communist terrorists in that country.

On Friday 11 March 1955 the *Eagle's* ship's company, headed by the Royal Marine detachment and band, marched from the Naval barracks at Devonport to 5 & 6 wharves where the *Eagle* now lay, and Captain Lewin took the salute. That afternoon the ship was commissioned at Ceremonial Divisions which were held in the lower hangar and Captain Lewin addressed the ship's company. Next day, at 11am, Divisions were again held in the lower hangar and, in the presence of the Lord Mayor of Exeter, a Dedication Service was conducted by the Chaplain of the Fleet, the Venerable F. N. Chamberlain. Following the ceremony there still remained a great deal to do to get the ship cleaned up and ready for sea, and for the C-in-C's inspection which was taking place on 25 March. Four days after this, at 8.40am on Tuesday 29 March 1955, the *Eagle* slipped her berth at Devonport and, with full ceremony, she put to sea for flying trials in the Channel.

Throughout the whole of April the *Eagle* steamed up and down the Channel, between the Isle of Wight and the Channel Islands, carrying out flying trials with Sea Hawks, Sea Venoms, Wyverns and Avengers. Finally, on 26 April, she carried out heeling trials, followed by main machinery trials, before returning to Devonport on 29 April to prepare for service in the Mediterranean once again.

It was Monday 9 May 1955 when the *Eagle* put to sea once again and for four days she carried out further flying trials off the Isle of Wight. During the weekend of 14/15 May she anchored at Spithead and was visited by a number of VIPs including the Lord Mayor and Sheriff of Exeter and the C-in-C Portsmouth, Admiral of the Fleet Sir George Creasy. On Monday 16 May the *Eagle* weighed anchor and that evening the Fifth Sea Lord, Rear-Admiral A. N. C. Bingley, who, during 1952-53 had been the ship's commanding officer, embarked by helicopter in order to witness the flying operations next day. 'Flying Stations' was piped at 7am on Tuesday 17 May, and by 7.30am four Sea Hawks and four Wyverns had been ranged for launching. Operations went without any untoward incidents and at 9.30am the four Wyverns of 827 Squadron prepared to land on once again. However, to everyone's horror, the first of these aircraft overshot the arrester wires and in attempting to take off again, it crashed into the base of the funnel leaving the engine firmly embedded in the ship's superstructure, while the fuselage fell back onto the flight deck. Fortunately there had been no spectators on the

During the *Eagle's* first long refit the biggest single task was to fit the carrier with an interim 5¹/₂° angled flight deck. This view shows the new deck with Sea Venoms, Sea Hawks and Wyverns ranged. *(Fleet Air Arm Museum)*

During the morning of Tuesday 17 May 1955, whilst carrying out flying trials off the Isle of Wight, a Wyvern crashed into the base of the *Eagle's* funnel. This view shows the damage caused and the wreckage being cleared away.

(Fleet Air Arm Museum)

goofing deck and there were no casualties on board and, miraculously, the pilot of the Wyvern survived, which indicates just how strongly built the aircraft was. With flying operations suspended and the remaining Wyverns diverted to RNAS Ford, the remains of the wrecked aircraft were ditched over the starboard side of the ship. Apparently Admiral Bingley had seen enough, for he left by helicopter and it was late afternoon before flying operations could begin again with the squadrons returning to their various stations.

Next morning, instead of leaving UK waters for the Mediterranean, the *Eagle* made a ceremonial entry into Portsmouth Harbour and was berthed alongside South Railway Jetty for repairs to her damaged funnel and island superstructure. This unscheduled 17-day stay in Portsmouth proved to be very popular with the ship's company, and on the last weekend in May, which included the Bank Holiday, the ship was a major attraction for thousands of visitors to Navy Days.

At just after noon on Saturday 4 June 1955, with all the repairs completed, the *Eagle* left Portsmouth and after embarking her squadrons and carrying out flying exercises in the Channel, she set course for Gibraltar where she arrived with full ceremony on the morning of Monday 13 June. From Gibraltar the *Eagle* steamed into the Mediterranean for Malta, arriving off the island on 18 June. The next eight days were spent carrying out intensive flying exercises off Malta, before the *Eagle* entered Grand Harbour and was berthed alongside Parlatorio Wharf to undertake a three-week self-maintenance period. After leaving Malta on 18 July there followed another 18 days of intensive exercises, relieved by a weekend anchored in Catania Bay, Sicily, during which time recreational leave was granted. Unfortunately, the break was marred by the accidental drowning of Ordinary Seaman J. A. Cameron, and when the *Eagle* was back at sea again on Monday 25 July his funeral service was held. On Friday 29 July the *Eagle* made a ceremonial entry into Grand Harbour, where she was secured to 11 & 11a buoys in Bighi Bay and next morning, at 9.30am, she hoisted the flag of Rear-Admiral

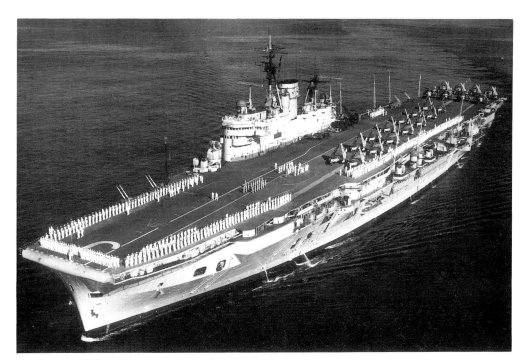

With repairs to the funnel completed, the *Eagle* sailed for the Mediterranean. Here she is shown arriving at Gibraltar on Monday 13 June 1955. *(N. Sims)*

At speed in the Mediterranean. *(N. Sims)*

On 4 August 1955, the day before *Eagle* visited Naples, a special 'family tree' photograph of the ship was taken by 'Baron', the society photographer. *(Fleet Air Arm Museum)*

Divisions on the flight deck at Malta.   (N. Sims)

A. Pedder, Flag Officer Aircraft Carriers (the appointment having replaced that of Flag Officer Heavy Squadron).

It was not long before the *Eagle* was at sea once again and she left Malta at 7.30am on Tuesday 2 August 1955 with the society photographer 'Baron' embarked, to take photographs of the ship for the *Illustrated London News*. Next day the C-in-C Mediterranean Fleet, Admiral Sir Guy Grantham, together with the Governor of Malta, Sir Robert Laycock, arrived by Gannet from Hal Far and during the afternoon the *Eagle*, the cruiser *Sheffield* and the Daring-class destroyers *Delight* and *Defender* carried out manoeuvres in the exercise area off Malta. That evening the two guests left the ship by air for Malta and the *Eagle* set course for Naples where she was to make an official visit. The following afternoon, as the ship's company prepared for her ceremonial entry into the Italian port, the carrier's speed was reduced to eight knots and 'Baron' was flown over the ship to take his photographs, which were described as *Eagle's* 'family tree'. At 9am on Friday 5 August 1955 the *Eagle* entered Naples Harbour, and after firing a 21-gun salute she was berthed alongside. There then followed a hectic seven-day visit during which time the ship was opened to visitors, numerous Italian VIPs were

entertained at official functions, and local children were treated to a party which they would always remember.

The visit ended at 9am on Friday 12 August 1955, when *Eagle* put to sea with a group of senior NATO officers on board who were to observe a flying display. One of the Wyverns from the ship crashed between the city of Naples and Mount Vesuvius but, fortunately, the pilot landed safely. That evening, with the flying exercises over, Captain Lewin took his ship right round the Isle of Capri, keeping as close inshore as he safely could, which must have been a magnificent sight for those on the island. Two days later the *Eagle* rendezvoused with HMS *Albion* off Malta and the two carriers took part in joint exercises with the US Sixth Fleet, including the aircraft carriers USS *Coral Sea* and USS *Intrepid*. During the exercises the *Eagle* lost a Sea Hawk, but fortunately the pilot was rescued safely.

At midday on Friday 19 August, the last day of the exercise, Sea Hawks from both the *Albion* and the *Eagle* performed a ceremonial fly-past over the US carriers before the two British ships left the area for Gibraltar. During the passage both the *Albion* and the *Eagle* carried out flying exercises and on Monday 22 August aircraft from the *Eagle* carried out 201 sorties, which was the largest number ever

Replenishment at sea during exercises off Invergordon, September 1955.   *(N. Sims)*

A fine aerial view of the *Eagle* taking on stores from an RFA during exercises in northern waters. The carrier's new interim angled flight deck is clearly visible.   *(Fleet Air Arm Museum)*

HMS *Eagle* leads *Centaur*, *Albion* and *Bulwark* into Trondheim Fjord on Wednesday 28 September 1955, on completion of exercises off Norway.   *(Fleet Air Arm Museum)*

flown by a British aircraft carrier on a single day and a tribute to the hard work put in by her ship's company. Two days later both carriers put into Gibraltar for a 15-day stay, before they left for Invergordon and the autumn exercises with the Home Fleet in the less hospitable waters off Norway.

During the voyage north the *Eagle* lost a Wyvern when the aircraft crashed into the sea, but the pilot, Lt Bush, bailed out and he was picked up by the SAR helicopter and safely landed on board. The two carriers arrived in the Cromarty Firth during the afternoon of Friday 16 September and the following day they were joined by the *Bulwark* and the *Centaur*, and the manoeuvres, which were primarily an anti-submarine exercise, started four days later. On the second day of the exercise Petty Officer Aircraft Handler F. Sale was killed when he was struck by the propeller blade of a Wyvern while directing aircraft into their deck parking positions. His funeral was held on Friday 23 September and two days later, on Sunday 25 September, Sub-Lt M. L. Teague RN of 827 Squadron lost his life when his Wyvern, which had developed a fuel leak, crashed whilst attempting an emergency landing on the *Bulwark*. Unfortunately he crashed into the sea and despite an intensive search, no trace of the pilot or his aircraft was found. Later that day a memorial service was held in the ship's chapel. On the morning of Tuesday 27 September one of the *Eagle's* helicopters ditched into the sea when taking off from the *Bulwark*, but fortunately two of the crew were picked up by the host ship's SAR helicopter, and one by the *Albion's*.

The exercise ended on Wednesday 28 September and that evening all four carriers anchored in Trondheim Fjord for a 'critique' on the exercises. Next morning, at 9am, HRH The Crown Prince of Norway, accompanied by the C-in-C Home Fleet, embarked to chair the conference which lasted for four hours. However, that afternoon the weather deteriorated, and with strong winds blowing across the anchorage the *Eagle* was forced to weigh anchor and steam down the Norwegian coast then through the Skagerrak to Oslofjord where she anchored off the capital city on the first day of October. During the nine-day visit the ship's football and cross-country running teams were put through their paces. Two days after *Eagle's* arrival off Oslo the *Centaur* arrived in the port and with her shallower draught she was able to go alongside. On 10 October, after embarking the British Ambassador to Norway, together with a number of foreign Naval Attachés, the *Eagle*, accompanied by the *Centaur*, left Oslo for Rosyth and whilst en route they rendezvoused with the *Albion*, which had left Copenhagen after an official visit. Together the three ships carried out a series of displays for the visitors, but for the *Eagle* the occasion was marred by the loss of another pilot. At 11.40am on Tuesday 11 October, a Wyvern being flown by Lt-Cdr L. P. Watson RN, the senior pilot of 827 Squadron, ditched over the ship's bow

after being launched from the port catapult. Within minutes the *Centaur's* SAR helicopter had recovered the pilot but, sadly, he was declared dead when brought back on board. After another full day of exercises all three carriers anchored off Rosyth on Thursday 13 October, and soon afterwards Lt-Cdr Watson's body was landed for the funeral service.

After ten days at Rosyth the *Eagle*, *Albion* and *Centaur* put to sea and rendezvoused with the *Bulwark*, which had steamed up the North Sea from Spithead, for 'Phoenix One', an exercise that was designed to test the ability of carrier-borne aircraft to intercept and deal with high altitude bombers. The exercise lasted for six days which, in the severe weather of the North Sea, was long enough for all those involved, and in the early hours of Saturday 29 October it was concluded when all the ships anchored off Rosyth. The *Eagle's* return to sea on Tuesday 1 November marked the final deployment of the first year of the commission and she returned to Devonport, arriving alongside 5 & 6 berths three days later. She went to sea for four days later that month to put on a series of 'Shop Window' displays for 45 visitors from the Ministry of Supply and the aircraft industry. The main purpose of the displays was to demonstrate various aspects of carrier operation, and in particular the arming and launching of aircraft in quick time. After embarking the visitors by helicopter at 8.15am and getting them into their goofing positions - complete with duffel coats - 23 Sea Hawks, all armed with an operational load of rockets, were launched. Then Wyverns, armed with 500lb bombs and rockets, and Gannets armed with depth charges and marine markers were ranged, while the Sea Hawks attacked a splash target towed astern. When the second launch was completed, the Sea Hawks were all recovered and refuelled ready for disembarkation. This was followed by the recovery of Wyverns and Gannets which had been bombing and depth charging smoke floats. All the aircraft were then refuelled and prepared for disembarkation, which was completed by 2.30pm. Between 10.30am and 2.30pm, with a break of just over an hour and a half for lunch, 81 aircraft sorties had been launched, half of them with operational loads. It was clear that the *Eagle* could easily beat her own record of 201 sorties a day whenever she pleased. The demonstration had proved a fitting conclusion to the first part of the *Eagle's* General Service Commission, and it had certainly impressed the visitors, some of whom commented that the organization and flying was better than anything they had seen the RAF do.

The next day, Friday 18 November 1955, whilst moored at C buoy in Plymouth Sound, FOAC inspected the ship and Ceremonial Divisions and was well satisfied with both. Four days later the *Eagle* slipped her mooring and steamed up-harbour to secure alongside 6 & 7 wharves of Devonport Dockyard. Ahead lay seasonal leave and a three-month docking period.

Chapter Six

Second Commission - 'Operation Musketeer'

On the last day of January 1956, with the *Eagle* lying in No 10 dry dock of Devonport Dockyard, Captain Lewin relinquished command of the ship to take up an appointment at the Admiralty and Captain H. C. D. MacLean DSC RN took over as commanding officer. Captain MacLean had joined the Navy in 1926 and during the Second World War he had served in HMS *Cossack*, and he was present when the *Altmark* was boarded. For his services in this action he was Mentioned in Dispatches. His next appointment was to HMS *Ark Royal* and he served in her until she was sunk in November 1941, and during this time he was awarded the Distinguished Service Cross.

On 6 February the C-in-C Plymouth, Admiral Sir Mark Pizey KBE CB DSO, visited the ship and 14 days later the *Eagle* was moved from the dry dock and berthed alongside 5 & 6 wharves and the ship's company were able to move back on board. However, it was Friday 6 April before the *Eagle* was ready for sea once again and she then left her berth to steam out to Plymouth Sound for the night before putting to sea the next day for four days of trials. After these had been completed successfully she returned to Devonport Dockyard where the squadron personnel joined the ship and ammunition was embarked. It was the morning of Monday 16 April 1956 when, with full ceremony the *Eagle* finally left Devonport, and over the next two days all the squadrons, which were 897 and 899 Sea Hawk Squadrons, 893 Sea Venom Squadron, 830 Wyvern Squadron, together with 812 Gannet Squadron (which she was actually taking out to Hal Far, Malta), and 849 Skyraider Squadron, were embarked. After two further days of flying exercises, during which time FOAC, Rear-Admiral A. Pedder, flew on board and hoisted his flag, the *Eagle* left UK waters and set course for Gibraltar where she arrived with full ceremony on Monday 23 April. Two days later she put to sea with the Governor of Gibraltar, Lieutenant-General Sir Harold Redman and the Flag Officer Gibraltar on board, and 897 and 899 Squadrons put on an impressive display over the ship. The two guests left the ship by helicopter that same afternoon and after two more days of exercises in the area, the *Eagle* set course for Malta, arriving off the island at the end of the month. There then followed eight days of intensive flying training, broken only by a weekend anchored at Pozzala Bay, Sicily, for recreational leave. After weighing anchor the *Eagle* returned to the exercise area off Malta where she rendezvoused with the *Albion* and *Centaur*, which were both homeward bound after having been deployed on the Far East Station. That afternoon aircraft from all three carriers performed a 'Grand Fly-Past' over Valletta. As the two smaller carriers left the area for Gibraltar, the *Eagle* made a ceremonial entry into Grand Harbour to secure at No 13 buoy in Bighi Bay.

On Monday 14 May Rear-Admiral A. Pedder struck his flag as FOAC, to return home to promotion and his final tour of duty as the Naval Commander of NATO's northern region, based at Oslo. That same day the new FOAC, Rear-Admiral M. L. Power, embarked and he hoisted his flag the next morning.

The *Eagle* left Grand Harbour on the morning of Tuesday 22 May

HMS *Eagle* in April 1956. *(Fleet Air Arm Museum)*

The *Eagle* makes a splendid sight as she enters Malta's Grand Harbour on the morning of Tuesday 8 May 1956.

(M. Kettle)

In late June 1956, during 'Exercise Thunderhead', the *Eagle* took part in damage control exercises and was listed 15° to starboard. Looking forward...

...and aft. *(N. Sims)*

1956, flying the flag of the First Sea Lord, Admiral of the Fleet Sir Algernon Willis, for the day, and she began to embark the squadrons from Hal Far. That afternoon as two Wyverns and eight Sea Hawks prepared to land, there was a tragedy when one Wyvern ditched in the sea. Within ten minutes the seaboat had been slipped but the pilot, Lt J. P. Smith RN, was found to be dead. With all flying suspended for the day it was next morning before the remainder of the aircraft could be embarked, and when this was completed the funeral service was held for Lt Smith. There then followed two days of intensive flying which continued until 10.30pm each evening before, on Saturday 26 May, the *Eagle* anchored at Syracuse, Sicily, for the weekend. The end of May 1956 saw the *Eagle* moored, once again, at No 13 buoy, Grand Harbour, to prepare for the summer cruise and exercises with the US Sixth Fleet.

Meanwhile, as the *Eagle* had been preparing for the second half of her commission, troop transports had been plying the Mediterranean as British troops were withdrawn from the Suez Canal Zone, under an agreement which had been signed on 19 October 1954. The agreement with the Egyptian Government provided for the withdrawal of British troops over a period of 20 months, and it brought to an end a period of vicious terrorist activity which, in 33 months, had cost the lives of 54 British servicemen. However, the agreement provided for the retention of workshop facilities at Tel-el-Kebir, west of Ismailia, and there were clauses which, under certain circumstances, provided for a British reoccupation of the Suez Canal Zone. The main body of fighting troops, the 2nd Battalion Grenadier Guards, had departed unobtrusively during the night of 24/25 March 1956, leaving behind a small rearguard who left by air two days later. It seemed that the thorny problem of Britain's military presence in Egypt had been resolved to everyone's satisfaction.

However, Arab nationalism was not solely confined to diplomatic relations between the Arabs and European powers, and there was only one issue which united the various Arab states: their bitter hatred of the state of Israel which had inflicted a crushing defeat on her Arab neighbours in 1948. By early 1956 tensions between Israel and the Arabs had almost reached breaking point and hardly a week went by without reports of serious military incidents along Israel's borders.

With hindsight perhaps it seems irrational that Britain should have felt herself responsible for the fate of the Suez Canal, for the Suez Canal Company never owned the canal, which originally belonged to the Ottoman rulers and subsequently to the Egyptian government. It was a joint stock company which had a concession to operate the waterway until November 1968 when it would revert to the Egyptians and Britain's purchase of forty-four per cent of the shares only entitled it to three directors on a board of 32. However, it was a sentiment born of history. Twice in the space of 50 years Britain had defended Egypt against invasion, first against the Turks in the first few months of 1915 and later, against the Italians and Germans during the Second World War. If Britain's position in the Middle East during the mid-1950s is to be fully understood then these events must be seen in context with her commercial interests in the region, which revolved around the supply of oil. In 1956 the Middle East was the source of most of the oil used by Britain, and the Suez Canal was the gateway to the area's rich oilfields.

Following the signing of the Anglo-Egyptian Treaty of October 1954 the USA, whose government was anxious to cultivate its own defence agreements, offered military aid to Egypt. However, in view of American support for the Baghdad Pact (a defence treaty signed by the United Kingdom, Turkey, Iraq, Iran and Pakistan), President Nasser of Egypt refused the offer. In 1955, with tensions growing between Egypt and Israel, Nasser changed his mind and decided to request military aid from the USA, but he was unable to meet the payment terms and unwilling to accept the fact that US military advisers would accompany the arms, and the deal fell through. In June 1955 Nasser approached the Soviet Union and a deal was struck between Egypt and Czechoslovakia. This provided for the supply of Russian T-34 tanks, self-propelled guns, artillery, rocket launchers, mortars and rifles, but, most important of all, MiG-15 jet fighters and Ilyushin jet bombers. By late 1955, with the delivery of this formidable arsenal under way, Nasser felt he could adopt an even more militant posture with regard to Israel.

In October 1955 Nasser moved troops to a demilitarized zone which controlled a strategic junction for Gaza, and Israel attacked an Egyptian frontier post in Gaza. The Israeli Government was becoming very anxious about the Czech arms which posed a major threat to their country's security, and a few weeks later the Israeli Prime Minister instructed his Chief of Staff, Brigadier-General Moshe Dayan, to be prepared to capture the Straits of Tiran at very short notice in order to ensure the free passage of Israeli shipping through the Gulf of Aqaba. In December 1955 Britain and the USA offered to pay the foreign exchange costs of Nasser's projected dam at Aswan on the River Nile, with additional financial support being provided by the World Bank. In return Nasser would have to back Western foreign policy in the Middle East but, with the Soviets hinting strongly that they might be

On the afternoon of Wednesday 25 July 1956, whilst the ship was at Naples, Gracie Fields entertained the ship's company on the flight deck. On the following day President Nasser of Egypt announced the nationalization of the Suez Canal.

(N. Sims)

At 9.20am on Friday 28 September 1956 the *Eagle* arrived at Toulon. Here she is shown going alongside at the French naval base, with the French carrier *Arromanches* (ex-*Colossus*) berthed nearby.

(Fleet Air Arm Museum)

prepared to back the project with no political strings attached, he refused the Anglo-American offer. In May 1956 there were rumours that Russia had offered Nasser a £50 million interest free loan, and by that time both the United States and Britain had doubts as to Egypt's ability to repay any loan. In the spring of 1956 Britain, although remaining pro-Arab in her Middle Eastern policy, realized that there was little chance of conciliation with Nasser and politically the situation was potentially dangerous. However, as the *Eagle's* summer cruise got under way there seemed to be little cause for any immediate concern.

On Saturday 2 June 1956 the *Eagle,* together with HMS *Birmingham,* flying the flag of the C-in-C Mediterranean Fleet, Admiral Sir Guy Grantham GCB CBE DSO, accompanied by HM Ships *Manxman, Diamond and Duchess,* left Malta for Istanbul. Three days later, as they approached the Dardanelles, the C-in-C transferred his flag to *Eagle* and later that day the carrier led the column into the Turkish waterway. Next day, after firing a national salute, the five ships anchored off the city of Istanbul for what was a short, but popular, five-day visit. During the time in port the ship's company put on the traditional children's party and when *Eagle* was opened to the public, despite the fact that visitors had to be ferried out by tender, almost 1,000 people looked round the ship in a space of just three hours. The visit ended at 4pm on Monday 11 June, when the ships weighed anchor and set courses through the Sea of Marmara and the Dardanelles, to the Aegean Sea. For the *Eagle* and *Birmingham* the next official visit was to Beirut which, at that time, 40 years ago, was still the wealthiest city in the Arab world and the epitome of stability. When the *Eagle* was off Cyprus a political adviser on Arab affairs from the Foreign Office joined the ship and at 11am on Friday 15 June both the *Eagle* and the *Birmingham* secured alongside the jetty in Beirut Harbour for a visit which was particularly important in view of the political tensions which were building up in the Middle East.

On a lighter note, a notice had appeared on the *Eagle's* main noticeboard asking for volunteers to take part in a camel ride from Beirut to Damascus. Apparently, so many members of the ship's company put their names to the list to be measured for 'camel stirrups', 'desert packed lunches' and for inoculations against 'camel bites' that the Commander had to put a stop to the prank. However, not to be deterred, the organizers posted notices that, although the ride was off, arrangements were in hand to have a Sheikh come on board to give a lecture on the 'cancelled' adventure. Although no firm arrangement was made, it is said that on the first evening of the stay in Beirut the *Eagle's*

HMS *Eagle* off Malta on 10 October 1956 as she undertook intensive flying exercises prior to 'Operation Musketeer'. *(Fleet Air Arm Museum)*

cable deck was crowded with interested members of the ship's company who had taken up mess stools and were patiently awaiting the arrival of the 'Sheikh'. The sheer numbers of those interested took the perpetrators by surprise and it is said that the Second Officer of the Watch had to face the throng with explanations. Rumours at the time pointed to a CPO Gunnery Instructor as being the chief organizer of the pranks.

As always during foreign visits there was a children's party and this time, when the ship was opened to visitors, nearly 1,400 people took the opportunity to look round in the space of an afternoon. On the diplomatic front Sir Guy Grantham hosted a reception for senior Lebanese Government ministers and on leaving the port, on the morning of Tuesday 19 June 1956, the President of Lebanon was embarked and given a flying demonstration.

HMS *Eagle* leads *Bulwark* and *Albion* during exercises in October 1956. *(Fleet Air Arm Museum)*

Then at just before midday, the *Eagle* steamed to within a mile of the Lebanese shore where the President disembarked into a launch and the *Eagle*, with her first social calls of the summer season concluded, proceeded for more serious business in the form of a major NATO air defence exercise with the US Sixth Fleet in the Gulf of Genoa.

The *Eagle* passed through the Strait of Bonifacio on the evening of Sunday 24 June 1956, and 'Exercise Thunderhead' started the next morning, with the US Sixth Fleet and its Essex-class carrier USS *Ticonderoga*. The exercise took place south of Toulon in severe weather and the *Eagle* lost two Sea Hawks, but fortunately both pilots were picked up safely and, on the last day of the month, with the exercise completed, *Eagle* again secured to No 11 buoy in Grand Harbour's Bighi Bay for a two-week self-maintenance period.

It was on the morning of 17 July that the *Eagle* put to sea once again, this time for the annual defence of Malta exercise 'Maltex 56', which took place in the Tyrrhenian Sea with the Sixth Fleet and the US carriers *Intrepid* and *Ticonderoga*. During the exercise two US aircraft were lost east of Stromboli. On the last day of the exercise a number of US Navy Banshees, Cougars and Cutlasses were put through their paces on the *Eagle's* flight deck, and for most of the pilots it was their first experience of the angled flight deck and the mirror landing sight. At 9am on Tuesday 24 July 1956, on conclusion of the exercise, the *Eagle* made a ceremonial entry into Naples for a short visit to the Italian city. The following morning a group of ship's company members left for a visit to Rome and an audience with the Pope, and in the afternoon Gracie Fields entertained the ship's company on the flight deck, which tended to overshadow a visit by the US Secretary for the Navy.

Next day, Thursday 26 July 1956, President Nasser of Egypt delivered a speech to a vast crowd assembled in Alexandria's Liberation Square, in which he proclaimed the Egyptian Government's decision to nationalize the Suez Canal Company, and within hours Egyptian Police and troops had seized control of the company's Egyptian offices. With the seizures came a declaration of martial law in the Canal Zone and orders for all employees of the company, including foreign nationals, to remain at their posts. This precipitous action had been brought about by the withdrawal of the USA and Britain from Nasser's Aswan project and, more surprisingly, by the Soviet denial that they had ever promised any financial assistance. For Nasser, who was determined to build a dam at Aswan, the only other source of revenue was from the Suez Canal and he could not turn back now.

At speed during the Suez campaign, 'Operation Musketeer'. The aircraft all bear the distinctive Allied striped markings. *(Fleet Air Arm Museum)*

In London and Paris the first government reaction to Nasser's proclamation was one of expected militancy. For the British Government it was really a matter of prestige, and for the French it was a question of ownership, for there was a distinct feeling that the Suez Canal was, in fact, theirs. On 27 July 1956, at a meeting between the Cabinet and Chiefs of Staff in London, the first ideas of military action against Egypt were discussed and a few days later senior French military officers arrived in London to discuss a joint operation.

The most powerful unit of both the British and French Mediterranean Fleets was HMS *Eagle*, and she was the only British carrier in the region at the time of Nasser's speech. The two French carriers *La Fayette* and *Arromanches*, (the former being the ex-USS *Langley*, an 11,000-ton Independence-class carrier, and the latter being the ex-HMS *Colossus*, the name ship of the light fleet carrier class), both operated piston-engined Corsairs and Avengers. However, neither the Sea Hawk nor the Sea Venom would be a match for the MiG-15s and, indeed, the only British fighters which would fit the bill were the RAF's Hawker Hunters and they were all based in the UK. Although the *Eagle* could be on station off Egypt very quickly, it was clear that any invasion of a country as vast as Egypt could not be undertaken at the drop of a hat and the Prime Minister, Sir Anthony Eden, did not want any risks to be taken. It would be necessary to make lengthy and extensive preparations, and in the meantime it was hoped that diplomatic efforts might resolve the situation.

On Sunday 29 July Captain MacLean addressed the ship's company and made it clear that, in the weeks and months ahead, the ship and the squadrons would be undergoing intensive training, and the following morning the *Eagle* left Naples for five days of flying exercises off Malta. During this period the squadrons, including 892 Sea Venom Squadron which had flown out from the UK, underwent an intensive night-flying work-up which, at its conclusion, left only the Wyverns unable to operate from the deck at night. On 6 August there was an eight-day break when the *Eagle* put into Grand Harbour for a further self-maintenance period. It is interesting to note that also moored in Grand Harbour at the time was the Egyptian destroyer *Ibrahim-el-Awal* (the ex-Hunt-class HMS *Mendip*), and shortly before the end of the *Eagle's* stay HMS *Bulwark* arrived in the Mediterranean from Portsmouth.

The *Eagle* left Malta once again on the morning of Tuesday 14 August and straightaway the intensive flying exercises started up again. Two days later, at just after midnight, 'Flying Stations' was piped and soon operations were under way with the Sea Hawks of 897 and 899 Squadrons, but at just after 2am tragedy struck when an aircraft of 897 Squadron ditched shortly after being launched. Immediately the *Eagle's* searchlights were switched on and the search for the downed aircraft began. Over three hours later the wrecked fuselage of the Sea Hawk was located, still afloat, but the pilot, Sub-Lt J. G. N. White RN, had not survived the accident and his body was recovered by the seaboat. After salvaging the wreckage of the Sea Hawk the funeral service was held for Sub-Lt White, and later that morning the *Eagle* joined the *Bulwark* at the Marsaxlokk anchorage.

The respite was only brief and next day both *Eagle* and *Bulwark* were at sea again and carrying out round-the-clock flying operations. However, on Saturday 25 August both ships put into Grand Harbour for a ten-day break before the next round of exercises started. When the *Eagle* and

Bulwark put to sea again on the morning of Tuesday 4 September they each had on board a French liaison officer, which indicated that joint training with the French would soon begin. Initially though the squadrons were employed in support of amphibious landing operations which were being practised round Malta, then after 16 days which included a very brief stay of 36 hours at Syracuse and eight days in Grand Harbour, both British carriers steamed north-west to the Gulf of Lyons for exercises with the French carriers *La Fayette* and *Arromanches*. Whilst en route, and just south of Sardinia, they rendezvoused with the *Albion* which had just cut short a refit in order to join them and reinforce the Navy's carrier force in the Mediterranean. During the training exercises a dawn strike on the French carriers by aircraft from both *Eagle* and *Bulwark* was a topic for much discussion amongst the French aviators and it was even rumoured that the *La Fayette's* Commander (Air) had been woken by the sound of aircraft attacking his ship.

On 26 September both the *Eagle* and *Bulwark* took a break from flying operations with the former putting in to the French naval base at Toulon while the latter made a visit to Marseilles. The popularity of the *Eagle's* visit to Toulon can be judged by the fact that on the first night some 1,200 of the ship's company went ashore and there was little sign of life in the wardroom. A coach trip was organized to an inland village of St Maxim, and a 19-strong party undertook a camping expedition to the St Baume mountain area 20 miles away. This gallant group pitched camp near a hotel where a very convivial '*entente cordiale*' was struck up in the bar.

However, the welcome six-day break was soon over and on Tuesday 2 October the *Eagle* put to sea again. Over the next three weeks the British carriers operated together in the Malta exercise area, with *Eagle* and *Bulwark* taking a short break at Gibraltar for maintenance. On board *Eagle* problems had been experienced with the starboard catapult which had been unserviceable for a day earlier in the month. However, upon leaving Gibraltar it was found that the problem remained and the flight deck engineers had to work hard to rectify the fault. On Thursday 25 October the *Eagle* put in to Grand Harbour and when she, *Albion* and *Bulwark* left on the morning of Monday 29 October 1956 the contemporary Press reports read: 'The aircraft carriers *Eagle*, *Albion* and *Bulwark* left here this morning with other naval units for an undisclosed destination.'

In fact the three carriers each undertook independent flying exercises off Malta, during which one of *Eagle's* Sea Hawks crashed on take-off but fortunately the pilot, Lt Middleton, was picked up safely. The exercises were

on zigzag courses as they approached the operating area 'Alfa', namely a circle of 35 miles radius with its centre at Lat 32° - 40'N/Long 31° - 20'E, about 330°and 95miles from Port Said. The three British carriers operated from the southern part of this area while the two French carriers remained in the northern region. At 3pm on 31 October it was announced that operations against military targets in Egypt had been ordered, and at 2.40am on the morning of Thursday 1 November flying operations by the British carriers commenced when one of *Eagle's* Skyraiders was launched on a reconnaissance flight round the force to ensure that the area was clear of Egyptian naval ships. Two hours later Sea Venoms took off on CAP duties and at 5.20am *Eagle* initiated the first strike of the operation when 12 Sea Hawks and six Sea Venoms were launched, their target being Inchass Airfield in the Nile Delta north-east of Cairo. Only meagre flak was experienced, and during the day 135 sorties were launched from the *Eagle*, their targets being the airfields at Bilbeis, Dekheila and Cairo West. As before anti-aircraft fire was light and at no time did they encounter any airborne opposition. Strikes were also flown against the blockship *Akka* which was moored in Lake Timsah and it was hit by at least one 500lb bomb. However, subsequent reconnaissance showed that the Egyptians were still trying to tow the *Akka* into position on the south side of the Canal and a further strike was flown by *Eagle's* Sea Hawks, as a result of which another direct hit was observed, although the *Akka* was subsequently sunk right across the buoyed channel of Lake Timsah.

completed at 10am on 30 October and after replenishing from RFA *Wave Sovereign* some 20 miles south of Crete, aircrew were briefed at 2pm and issued with pistols, escape and evasion packs and khaki clothing. At just before 9pm the *Eagle* joined the main British force which, together with *Albion* and *Bulwark*, also included HM Ships *Ceylon* and *Jamaica*, as well as HMNZS *Royalist*, *Diamond* and *Duchess*, and by 11pm all the aircraft had been armed.

At 4.30pm on Monday 29 October 1956, the Israeli Army had started its assault on Egyptian forces in Sinai and over the following 24 hours they had made rapid progress as they advanced towards the vitally strategic Mitla Pass. At 4.15pm on Tuesday 30 October, Sir Anthony Eden announced the terms of an 'urgent communication' to both Egypt and Israel stating that they should cease fire and pull back to positions no closer than ten miles to the Suez canal on either side. Egypt was also to allow an Anglo-French force to move temporarily into positions along the canal. The message went on to say that, failing Egyptian consent, 'British and French forces will intervene in whatever strength may be necessary to secure compliance.' It was obvious that, with the Israelis advancing rapidly across the Sinai, Egypt would not pull its troops ten miles to the west of the Suez Canal, nor would they agree to the occupation of the Canal Zone by the Anglo-French forces. As we now know the Israeli government was working in conjunction with both the British and French governments and so their response to the ultimatum made no difference at all. Thus the scene was set for an Anglo-French invasion of Port Said.

At 1.30am on Wednesday 31 October, the British Fleet switched off all navigation lights and commenced steaming

On Friday 2 November strikes continued against the airfields and during the afternoon when it became clear that the majority of aircraft left on the ground were either burned out or damaged, the target was moved to Huckstep Camp, a large Egyptian supply dump east of Cairo. Later reconnaissance photographs of this location showed all the hits in the target area with extensive damage to military vehicles which would have been used against the Allied landings scheduled for 5 November. During Friday one of 893 Squadron's Sea Venoms, which was attacking Almaza Airfield in the Nile Delta, was hit by flak and subsequently

Sea Venoms being launched from HMS *Eagle* against Egyptian targets. *(Fleet Air Arm Museum)*

suffered a complete hydraulic failure. Fortunately the pilot, Lt-Cdr Wilcox RN, made a perfect wheels up landing, but his observer suffered serious leg injuries which later resulted in the loss of his left leg above the knee.

On Saturday 3 November strikes on airfields in the Nile Delta continued, but the priority target was the Gamil Bridge as the Allied offensive switched to lines of communication. This bridge had to be destroyed to prevent Egyptian reinforcements coming in from the east. During one of these attacks a Wyvern flown by Lt D. F. McCarthy RN was hit by anti-aircraft fire, but he managed to fly his plane out over the coast where, losing height rapidly, he bailed out. Lt McCarthy then spent an uncomfortable time in his dinghy while the Egyptian garrison at Port Said shelled him. However, they were silenced by *Eagle's* Sea Hawks and Lt McCarthy was safely recovered by the ship's Whirlwind helicopter. By the end of the day five attacks had been made on the Gamil Bridge and a large section of it had been destroyed.

On Sunday 4 November *Eagle* withdrew from the operating area to replenish from the Underway Replenishment Group, and no flying was done other than the recovery of replacement aircraft which were flown in from RAF El Adam near Tobruk. Later that evening orders were received for the landing of British and French paratroops in the Port Said area, which was scheduled for 7.15am the following morning. At 5.30am on Monday 5 November *Eagle's* operations recommenced, providing close air support for the airborne landing, and during the later part of the morning the ship's helicopters came into their own by taking medical supplies to the paratroops at Gamil Airfield. They were also able to provide a shuttle service evacuating casualties. While operating in support of the paratroopers a Wyvern was hit by anti-aircraft fire, but the pilot, Lt-Cdr Cowling, managed to eject some ten miles offshore and, once again, a rapid recovery was made by the helicopters. At the end of that day FOAC received the following message from the Army commander ashore: 'To all supporting aircraft: many thanks for your magnificent support to us this day, which thrilled all ranks. Its timely effectiveness and accuracy were beyond praise and doubtless saved many casualties. Please convey our gratitude to all concerned.'

The main Allied seaborne landing was made on the morning of Tuesday 6 November and the ease with which it was accomplished speaks volumes for the air operations carried out by the Fleet Air Arm. Although *Eagle's* aircraft flew sorties in support of the assault forces from 5.30am through to 5.25pm, there were few calls for air strikes. During the afternoon armed reconnaissance sorties were flown along the whole length of the canal from Port Said to Suez, and during an attack on a squadron of Egyptian tanks near the Egyptian Army camp at El Kantara, Lt Donald Mills RN, had to eject from his Sea Hawk after being hit by flak. He actually landed on the west side of the canal not far from El Kantara, and during the time it took to fly the planeguard helicopter from the ship to rescue him, Sea Venoms from the *Albion* and French Corsairs kept up a constant patrol overhead.

By the end of flying operations on the afternoon of Tuesday 6 November the *Eagle's* port catapult was considered to be unsafe and, as the starboard catapult had been unserviceable throughout the operation, it was clear that the carrier could not participate in any further fixed-wing flying and the decision was made to send her back to Malta for repairs. In fact, at midnight on 6/7 November a ceasefire was to come into effect as the British and French governments, under international pressure, agreed to demands by the United Nations Secretary General for a cessation of hostilities with a UN force subsequently occupying the combat zone. And so the three carriers would not undertake any more air strikes, but CAPs would have to be maintained until all British troops had been safely withdrawn.

On the morning of 7 November FOAC transferred his flag and a proportion of his staff to the *Bulwark* and the *Eagle* set course for Malta, arriving in Grand Harbour on the morning of Friday 9 November. During the six days of 'Operation Musketeer', with only one of her catapults serviceable, the *Eagle* had flown over 650 sorties. The Egyptian Air Force was virtually destroyed, his armour had been severely damaged and his military airfields had been rendered unserviceable. The airborne landings on 5 November and the seaborne assault on 6 November had been given continuous air support. Strike aircraft had been directed onto targets by the Army ashore, so that any Egyptian resistance was swiftly crushed. With very little loss all objectives had been met, and when the ceasefire was announced, the Army had been poised for its sweep down the canal to Ismailia and Suez. There is no doubt that *Eagle* had acquitted herself well.

After four days in Malta, during which time both catapults were repaired, the *Eagle* put to sea again on the afternoon of Tuesday 13 November and set course for the Port Said area, where for the rest of the month her aircraft provided air patrols over the Suez Canal Zone while the Army withdrawal was under way. This period was marred by two tragic accidents, the first during the afternoon of Monday 19 November when NAM(O) C. A. Naylor was killed instantly in an explosion at the forward end of the lower hangar. The resulting fire also destroyed two aircraft and the hangar had to be sealed off while the firemain sprays were used to extinguish the blaze. The following afternoon the funeral service was held for NAM Naylor. The second accident, on Saturday 24 November, involved the loss of a Skyraider and its crew of three, Lt I. G. Elliot RN, Sub-Lt R. J. Connolly RN and Sub-Lt I. L. Beale RN. Next day a memorial service was held for the lost aircrew.

Also on Sunday 25 November *Eagle's* nylon crash barrier was put to use for the first time in the commission when a Sea Venom made a successful wheels up landing with only superficial damage. During this period, Lt-General Sir Hugh Stockwell KCB DSO, the commanding officer of the ground forces during the operations, visited the ship and addressed the ship's company. On 27 November the *Eagle* left the Port Said area to anchor briefly off Limassol, Cyprus, but on the following day she returned to Port Said once again. However, on 1 December the ship's company enjoyed a break from operations when the carrier secured to No 13 buoy in Grand Harbour's Bighi Bay.

The *Eagle* left Malta again on Tuesday 11 December 1956, once again bound for the waters off Port Said to cover the Army evacuation. That same afternoon the First Lord of the Admiralty, Lord Hailsham, and the Secretary of the Admiralty, Sir John Lang, embarked by helicopter to be briefed by Vice-Admiral Power. The following day they left the ship to visit the *Bulwark* and the *Albion*, and the *Eagle* relieved the former in order to complete the task of covering the British withdrawal from Port Said. On Christmas Eve the *Eagle* was still in the waters off the Levant and the commission, which had been due to be completed in early December, was clearly going to run into early 1957.

During the afternoon of Christmas Day the *Eagle* left the operational area to return to Malta and later the following afternoon the C-in-C Mediterranean, Admiral Sir Guy Grantham, embarked by helicopter to address the officers and ship's company, and to thank everyone for the enormous effort which had been put in during 'Operation Musketeer' and the subsequent withdrawal. After flying the Venoms of 893 Squadron to Hal Far and disembarking the C-in-C, the *Eagle* set courses for Gibraltar and home. She made a full ceremonial entry into Gibraltar on the morning of Saturday 29 December for a three-day stay, and on New Year's Day 1957, after Vice-Admiral Power had hauled down his flag, the *Eagle* left her berth alongside the South Mole and set course for Devonport. Two days later all serviceable aircraft were launched to their respective stations and at first light on Friday 4 January the *Eagle* was secured to C buoy in Plymouth Sound. During the next two days Customs formalities were completed and all squadron personnel were disembarked before, on the morning of Monday 7 January 1957, with full ceremony, the *Eagle* steamed up-harbour to berth alongside 5 & 6 wharves of Devonport Dockyard.

Perhaps the last word should go to the First Sea Lord, Admiral Lord Mountbatten, who wrote to Captain MacLean: 'In welcoming you back to England I want to congratulate you and your ship's company on the part you played in "Operation Musketeer".

Eagle was the linchpin on which the whole operation depended and it is hard to see how it could have taken place at all without you. In particular, I think that your performance in putting up over 600 sorties was very remarkable, in view of all the trouble you had with your catapult.

I fully realize the difficulties with which you and your ship's company had to compete and I am only sorry that we could not get you home in time for Christmas and the New Year.

With my best wishes to you and your ship's company for 1957.'

HMS *Eagle* in the Mediterranean, December 1956. *(Fleet Air Arm Museum)*

Chapter Seven

Third Commission - Return To The Med

Having been delayed by 'Operation Musketeer' and after returning home to Devonport late, the third commission started with the *Eagle* having only just been delivered into Dockyard hands, where she was due to remain for some months. On Monday 18 February 1957 Captain Michael Le Fanu DSC RN joined the ship and took over from Captain MacLean. Eight days later, on a cold, wet Tuesday, 1,500 members of the ship's company marched from the barracks to the ship where Captain Le Fanu took the salute and the *Eagle* was commissioned. The official ceremony was held on the morning of Thursday 28 February with the service being conducted by the Dean of Exeter, and following this the refit began in earnest when the *Eagle* was moved into No 10 dry dock. The next five months were most uncomfortable for the ship's company with dockyard cables, wires and hoses festooning the vessel,

and gaping holes everywhere following the removal of tank covers. At least with the ship working a dockyard routine, most men were able to get away each weekend.

The *Eagle* left the dry dock on 27 May and with the dockyard debris quickly cleared away, the carrier finally resembled a ship once again. The new commission coincided with an announcement from the Admiralty that the standard displacement tonnage of the *Eagle*, and her sister *Ark Royal*, had been reassessed and instead of the previous figure of 36,800 tons, it was now 43,340 tons, which ranked them as equals with the US Navy's Midway-class of aircraft carrier.

Sailing day finally arrived on Friday 5 July 1957 when, at 11.30am, the *Eagle* left her berth for the short journey to C buoy in Plymouth Sound where she was to embark aviation fuel. However, no sooner had the tanker started to

A fine bow view of the *Eagle* at speed. *(Fleet Air Arm Museum)*

Sea Hawks starting up.　　*(Fleet Air Arm Museum)*

pump the 'avgas', than a fire broke out in one of the carrier's boiler room fan flats. Because of the risk of explosion, the fuelling vessel, *Air Sprite*, stopped pumping and stood off while a fire-fighting tug of the city's fire brigade stood by in case it was required. Fortunately, the ship's own fire-fighting teams extinguished the blaze and the damage, which was only slight, did not affect the *Eagle's* operational efficiency. Next day the *Eagle* left Plymouth Sound and put to sea for her trials and shakedown cruise.

During the trials the personnel of 700 Squadron joined the ship and landing trials were carried out by the squadron's Sea Hawks. Ten days after leaving her home station, the *Eagle* was once again alongside 5 & 6 wharves at Devonport Dockyard to carry out catapult trials and to rectify machinery defects which had come to light. On 31 July a 'Families Day' was held for the ship's company, and on the following day the personnel of 803 and 806 Sea Hawk Squadrons and 813 Wyvern Squadron embarked.

The *Eagle* left Devonport during the morning of Friday 2 August 1957 and set course for Spithead for the embarkation of her aircraft. During the afternoon of 3 August the SAR helicopter ditched off the *Eagle's* starboard beam and a second helicopter was launched to rescue the

crew, who were returned on board safely. On the evening of 5 August, when the aircraft had been recovered safely, the *Eagle* set course for the north-east coast of Scotland, by way of the Dover Strait and the North Sea. The remainder of the month was spent exercising off Lossiemouth, but unfortunately the ship's company was hit by an outbreak of Asian Flu which was sweeping the country at that time. Despite the fact that large numbers of the ship's company were going down with the illness, flying operations continued, but when the *Eagle* secured to B buoy at Rosyth for a weekend break the ship was put under quarantine with leave being restricted to the playing fields at Rosyth and the naval canteen. Fortunately, no sooner had the quarantine been imposed than the epidemic waned and the leave restrictions could be lifted. At its worst some 200 men had been affected by the outbreak and many mess decks began to take on the appearance of hospital wards.

The *Eagle* left Rosyth on the morning of Tuesday 10 September for exercises off the north of Scotland. Laurence Moore, who was a Shipwright Artificer at the time, remembers: 'I joined the *Eagle* at Rosyth in the late summer of 1957, and my job as a 5th Class Shipwright Artificer was to assist the Shipwright to lower the Y beacon,

Captain Michael Le Fanu stirs the Christmas pudding as the 'flavouring' is added. *(Fleet Air Arm Museum)*

so that the *Eagle* could negotiate the Forth Railway Bridge safely as we left for "Exercise Strikeback".' *Eagle* joined the cruiser *Gambia*, the *Ark Royal* and the *Bulwark* and on Friday 13 September the ships anchored off Greenock for a long weekend, before leaving on Tuesday 17 September to participate in the NATO exercise. Over 100 ships were present, including the US Navy's giant carriers *Forrestal* and *Saratoga*, and the cruiser USS *Albany*. On leaving Greenock the fleet steamed north of the Arctic Circle from where aircraft from all the carriers carried out attacks on ground targets from northern Norway to Denmark. The *Eagle's* main task was to provide fighter defence and anti-submarine reconnaissance, but the strike and ground attack aircraft were also put through their paces. During one strike a Wyvern went out of control and the pilot was forced to eject, but he was safely picked up by a fishing boat. Another pilot ejected from his Sea Hawk which had caught fire and he was rescued by one of the *Bulwark's* helicopters. This favour was reciprocated when the *Eagle's* SAR helicopter picked up the crew of one of the *Bulwark's* Gannets which had been forced to ditch. Perhaps the

luckiest rescue of all was that of Petty Officer Davies who, at 10.35pm on Wednesday 25 September, a pitch-black night, fell overboard from 2M fuelling position just after the *Eagle* had fuelled from the RFA *Tiderange*. PO Davies was well muffled in oilskins and sea boots but the sea was rough at the time. The lifebuoy sentry acted very promptly and, although he could not see PO Davies, he threw a lifebuoy which landed only a few feet from the unfortunate petty officer. Luckily a nearby officer was actually on the telephone to the bridge at the time and, as he saw the incident happening, he was able to report 'man overboard' direct to the Officer of the Watch who pressed the lifebuoy buzzers, made the signal 'man overboard' to all ships and switched on lights to illuminate the surrounding area. HMS *Whirlwind*, which was two cables (365m) off *Eagle's* starboard quarter, immediately stopped from 20 knots and turned towards the lifebuoy. PO Davies was soon spotted in the beam of *Whirlwind's* searchlight and he was told by megaphone that help was on its way. The *Whirlwind* was then manoeuvred so that PO Davies was alongside the after end of her quarterdeck and he was able to climb to safety

A Sea Hawk is prepared for launching. *(Fleet Air Arm Museum)*

A Sea Hawk catches the wire. *(Fleet Air Arm Museum)*

The *Eagle* and the *Ark Royal* (nearest) together in Grand Harbour, February 1958.   *(A. J. Perrett)*

with the aid of a jumping ladder and heaving lines. Happily, apart from being very cold and wet, he was unhurt. There is no doubt that this well executed rescue was due to quick and efficient action being taken by all concerned, and a special commendation went to Marine Mahood for his very prompt action as lifebuoy sentry.

'Exercise Strikeback' ended on the morning of Saturday 28 September and two days later, on the last day of the month, the *Eagle* secured to C buoy in Plymouth Sound. Next day she steamed up-harbour to berth alongside 5 & 6 wharves and, to the relief of everyone on board, start a ten-day self-maintenance period.

When the *Eagle* left Devonport once again on Saturday 12 October 1957, another attempt was made to complete a night-flying programme which had been started off Lossiemouth during August that year but, as before, the schedule was ruined by severe weather conditions. In the early hours of Friday 18 October the *Eagle* left the Channel and steamed across the Bay of Biscay to Vigo, and the first foreign visit of the commission. On the following day the *Eagle* anchored in Vigo Bay just long enough to embark a party of Spanish defence officials and naval officers, before

putting to sea to stage a flying display. That same afternoon she returned to picturesque Vigo Bay where she anchored close to the transatlantic passenger terminal. During the eight-day stay in the Spanish port an enjoyable time was had by all, helped by the local vino, a favourable exchange rate and even dancing girls on the flight deck alongside the Sea Hawks. In return the ship's company hosted the traditional children's party, and the Royal Marines Beat Retreat, but in the early afternoon of Saturday 26 October it was time to start work once again as the *Eagle* put to sea to rendezvous with the *Ark Royal* and the *Albion* for joint flying exercises which enabled the night-flying work-up to be completed.

After spending 11 days alongside at Devonport the *Eagle* left her berth on the morning of Thursday 14 November 1957, bound for Rosyth and exercises with the Home Fleet. Sailing by way of the Dover Strait she arrived off Rosyth on the morning of 16 November, when the C-in-C Home Fleet, Admiral Sir John Eccles, and his staff embarked and hoisted his flag. The exercise 'Phoenix II', which also included both *Bulwark* and *Ark Royal*, started on the morning of 18 November, but with severe gales and

A magnificent aerial view of the *Eagle*, with Sea Hawks overhead. *(M. Kettle)*

heavy seas, flying was very difficult at times and it often had to be suspended altogether. With the flight deck moving up and down as much as 60ft on occasions it was a severe test for the pilots, but they performed admirably and came through without any casualties. The exercise ended on the morning of Saturday 23 November and to everyone's relief the three carriers returned to Rosyth that same day for a long weekend. The *Eagle* sailed again on 26 November and two days later she was secured alongside 5 & 6 wharves at Devonport Dockyard where she would remain for two months whilst the ship's company took seasonal leave, and routine maintenance was carried out.

On 5 December 1957 the *Eagle* became the flagship of FOAC, Rear-Admiral H. C. D. MacLean, the carrier's previous commanding officer, but he was only occupying this position for a short while and on Monday 6 January 1958 he was relieved by Vice-Admiral A. N. C. Bingley, who had been the ship's second commanding officer. It was also announced by the Admiralty that a refit which had been scheduled for the *Eagle* later in 1958 had been cancelled and that she would undergo an extensive

modernization programme during 1959 instead. This would include the installation of steam catapults which would be capable of launching the new Scimitar aircraft, and the work was expected to last for three years. As well as major alterations to the flight deck, important changes were proposed in the accommodation for the ship's company, including moving the wardroom one deck higher and rearranging most of the mess decks, several of which were to be fitted with bunks in place of hammocks.

After embarking the personnel from 803 and 806 Squadrons, 894 Sea Venom Squadron, 813 Wyvern Squadron, 814 Gannet Squadron and 849A Skyraider Flight, the *Eagle* left Devonport on the morning of Tuesday 28 January 1958 to rendezvous with the *Ark Royal* and the ships of the Dartmouth Training Squadron and to set courses for the Mediterranean. Tony Perrett, who was an Aircraft Artificer at the time serving with 814 Squadron, remembers joining the *Eagle* for the first time: 'We joined the *Eagle* from a snowbound RNAS Eglinton in Northern Ireland and, at first, I found the sheer size of the *Eagle* awesome and it took many weeks to find my way around her. Conditions on board were very cramped and even for us CPOs on 6D forward mess, living space was very limited. There were 65 of us on the mess deck and most of us slept in hammocks which, although basic, were quite comfortable and they were a "haven" for all those afflicted with bouts of seasickness. We were situated near the canteen flat and we used to gain access to the mess by going down through our dining hall. Later, when we were in the Mediterranean, the cable deck was a favourite place to sleep as it was open to the cool breezes and it was well below the flight deck. Space was so limited that many ratings used to have to sling their hammocks in the oddest of places when the mess decks were full. However, despite this, the *Eagle* was a happy ship.'

By early 1958, in the aftermath of Suez and with the rapid rise of Arab nationalism, it was clear that the Middle East was very unstable. President Nasser of Egypt had united his country with Sudan to form the United Arab Republic, and Jordan and Iraq were about to set up an alliance known as the Arab Federation. The political situation was further complicated by France's problems with its North African colony of Algeria and by Nasser's strident Arab nationalist propaganda which was being broadcast to all the countries in the region.

The arrival of the carriers and their escorts at Gibraltar on Friday 31 January 1958 filled the harbour, but their stopover lasted only for a weekend before they left for Malta. Whilst en route aircraft from both aircraft carriers took part in 'Exercise Febex' and on 7 February, as they arrived off Marsaxlokk, the squadrons from both *Eagle* and *Ark Royal* took part in a massed fly-past of 56 aircraft over Valletta. During the next seven days both carriers undertook intensive flying exercises off the coast of Libya, during the course of which the Gannets of 814 Squadron escorted the Turkish destroyer *Gemlik*, which was taking the Turkish president home from a visit to Tunisia. Finally, during the afternoon of Friday 14 February, the *Eagle* and the *Ark Royal* entered Grand Harbour and were berthed in Bighi Bay. Next day Captain J. B. Frewen RN joined the ship and at midday on Sunday 16 February he took command of the *Eagle* as Captain Le Fanu left the ship to return home to promotion and an appointment at the Admiralty. Captain Frewen had entered the service in 1924 as a cadet at the age of 13, and he had served as the navigating officer in the cruisers *Durban* and *London*, as well as in the aircraft carrier *Formidable*. He had been in the *Formidable* when she was the flagship of Rear-Admiral Sir Philip Vian during the final year of the Pacific War, and took part in attacks on Okinawa and Kyushu when the carrier was hit by two kamikaze aircraft.

After a ten-day self-maintenance period in Malta, the *Eagle* left Grand Harbour during the morning of Tuesday

The *Eagle* in the Mediterranean in 1958. *(M. Pack)*

25 February 1958, to carry out independent flying exercises before joining the rest of the Mediterranean Fleet. However, the flying programme got off to a bad start when, during the first afternoon, a Sea Hawk of 803 Squadron, piloted by Lt A. L. Mackintosh RN, ditched in the sea south of Malta. Despite an intensive search by the *Eagle* and the destroyer *Diana*, sadly no trace was found of the pilot or his aircraft. After six days of flying the *Eagle* joined the *Ark Royal* and other units of the Mediterranean Fleet, and the aircraft carriers *Saratoga* and *Essex* from the US Sixth Fleet. 'Exercise Marjex' got under way on 3 March and, for the *Eagle*, it almost started with a disaster. At about 11am that morning Commander Roberts, the commanding officer of 803 Squadron, was launched from the ship in a Sea Hawk. During the launch his cockpit canopy was smashed and both his auxiliary and main drogue parachutes were triggered as the aircraft went off the catapult. As he became airborne the parachutes wrapped around the tailplane but, with very skilful handling, Commander Roberts was able to land safely at Hal Far.

On completion of the exercise the carriers steamed north-west for the Bay of Hyeres but, in the early hours of 8 March, the *Eagle* was diverted to search for two French pilots whose aircraft had collided and ditched some 60 miles north of Cape Bon, Tunisia. The *Eagle* was the first ship to arrive in the area and for 18 hours, together with merchant ships and French naval units, she searched the seas off North Africa. As a result of the combined efforts one survivor was rescued, and at 7pm that evening *Eagle* resumed her voyage to the Bay of Hyeres, arriving there on the morning of 10 March to start trials of the French Navy's new aircraft, the three-seater Breguet Alizé anti-submarine plane and the lightweight two-seater twin jet Fouga Magister trainer. Despite four days of atrocious winter weather - when at times the ship had to steam astern at five knots to reduce the wind over the deck - the aircraft chalked up 93 catapult launchings and deck landings, and when the carrier finally anchored in Hyeres Roads on the evening of Thursday 13 March there were sighs of relief all round. Next morning, at 8.30am, the *Eagle* secured alongside in the French naval base at Toulon where, with strong winds still blowing, there was little room to manoeuvre and 'Operation Pinwheel', where the Wyverns and Gannets ran their engines on the flight deck to assist the turning of the ship, helped her to berth safely. During the stay Tony Perrett, and others, joined a coach trip along the Riviera to Monaco. It was shortly after Prince Albert was born and the principality was still celebrating the event. Following her six-day visit to Toulon the *Eagle* returned to Gibraltar and during the passage a member of the ship's company fell over the side, but the planeguard helicopter soon recovered him and returned him safely to the ship.

Following a short weekend break at Gibraltar, *Eagle* joined the NATO exercise 'Dawn Breeze', which most of the ship's company christened 'Full Gale' as the ship steamed into storm force winds and heavy seas in the Atlantic Ocean. During Thursday 27 March the storm caused damage to the ship's motor cutter and to the carley floats, but the following day, with the storm having abated somewhat, the Sea Hawks and Venoms were launched to intercept RAF Canberra and Valiant bombers. At the end of the exercise, on the afternoon of Saturday 29 March, the Wyverns of 813 Squadron were launched for the last time from a British aircraft carrier. The squadron commanding officer even acted as chief mourner when his Wyvern, which had been damaged, was committed to the deep with full 'military honours'. It was said that the departure of the Wyverns was accompanied by relief for *Eagle's* regular goofers, who had become rather nervous of the aircraft despite its good landing record. 803 Squadron also left the *Eagle* for good that day as they were disbanding, to re-form with Scimitars in place of Sea Hawks.

After the aircraft had flown off, the first ship's concert was held in the hangar and it proved to be a fitting climax to the first half of the commission for, next morning, the ship anchored in Cawsand Bay. Later that day, after Customs officers had done their worst, the *Eagle* weighed anchor and steamed up-harbour to berth alongside 7 & 8 wharves. The next day she was moved to No 10 dry dock where she remained until the end of April.

Chapter Eight

Third Commission - Royal Visitors

Even before the *Eagle* left dry dock on 1 May 1958, political tensions in the Middle East were again building up with anti-government disturbances in Lebanon and with problems for the French in Algeria, where a colonist insurrection was threatened. When the *Eagle* left Devonport on Tuesday 20 May, the national Press was already speculating that she would be bound for the eastern Mediterranean. That same afternoon the aircraft of 806 and 898 Sea Hawk Squadrons, 831B and 894 Sea Venom Squadrons, 814 Gannet Squadron and 849 Skyraider Squadron, together with the Whirlwind anti-submarine helicopters of 701 and 820 Squadrons, were embarked in Lyme Bay. After carrying out flying exercises the next day, the *Eagle* left UK waters once again and set course through a very rough Bay of Biscay for Gibraltar. Following a weekend at anchor in Gibraltar Bay the *Eagle* left for flying exercises, during which the 5,000th arrested deck landing of the commission was clocked up, and for her first foreign visit of the deployment, an official call at Barcelona. The visit began on the morning of Friday 30 May 1958, when the *Eagle* anchored off the Spanish port to embark the Mayor and Civil Governor of Barcelona, together with military officers, for a flying display which included an impressive aerobatic team of four Sea Hawks from 806 Squadron. Later that day the ship returned to Barcelona, where she anchored half a mile off the breakwater for the six-day visit. For some the main attraction of the stay in Barcelona was the International

Trade Fair or the architecture of the old buildings, while for others the cafés, restaurants and night clubs left indelible memories. In return the *Eagle* hosted a children's party and an official cocktail party, at which a British Cabinet Minister was a guest - a very unusual event in a foreign port. The highlight of the party was, without doubt, Beating Retreat by the Royal Marine Band. It was described in the local Press as, '...a retreat in which the Marines interpret military music and at the same time carry out artistic evolutions.'

From Barcelona the *Eagle* steamed east for Akrotiri Bay, Cyprus, where she was to relieve the *Ark Royal* on the Mediterranean Station. Unfortunately, the flying programme which had been planned for the passage had to be cancelled because of a breakdown in the evaporators, and water rationing had to be introduced. When Captain Frewen addressed the ship's company on the morning of 8 June there was more bad news. A proposed visit to Istanbul had been postponed and, instead, the *Eagle* would spend many weeks patrolling the coast of Cyprus where the EOKA terrorist campaign was at its height.

The *Eagle* anchored in Akrotiri Bay early on the morning of Tuesday 10 June and almost immediately the helicopters of 820 Squadron began to transfer all their stores and personnel from the *Ark Royal* in a shuttle service of 66 sorties, actually completing the job in less than two hours. Next day, as the *Eagle's* off-duty watches headed for banyans on the beaches outside Akrotiri, the *Ark Royal* weighed anchor and headed for home.

On the morning of Thursday 12 June, what could have been a disaster was prevented when, at 8.40am fire broke out in the oxygen plant on board the *Eagle*. Although he realized the danger to himself, ERA J. W. Rowden dashed back into the compartment and turned off the supply of oxygen to the plant. There is no doubt that ERA Rowden's brave action prevented what could have been a very serious explosion, and he received a commendation from the C-in-C. Meanwhile, the ship's company settled down to a routine which involved patrolling the waters off

The *Eagle* anchored off the breakwater at Barcelona in early June 1958. *(A. J. Perrett)*

In October 1958 the *Eagle* visited the ancient city of Istanbul, formerly Byzantium, and as Constantinople, capital of the Ottoman Empire. In this view her bows are facing the Dolmabahche Palace.   (M. Pack)

the coast of the Mediterranean island. Tony Perrett remembers those days: 'Life on board the *Eagle* was quite enjoyable and I used to do a regular spot on the ship's radio called, "Let's Go To A Show", in which I narrated the plot and played the music from musicals and films. I was also able to perform in the various concerts which were held in one of the hangars or, in the really hot weather, on the flight deck.' Laurence Moore also recalls those weeks when, 'We shipwrights had a very competitive deck hockey team and I, being left-handed, used to sneak in many a goal. We had some rough matches, particularly against a squadron team which included Lt P. Carmichael, a pilot who had been decorated for shooting down a MiG fighter in Korea. I also recall our banyan parties to the beach in Cyprus when the EOKA terror campaign was at its height. I was detailed off for duties as a beach sentry, and I was armed with a Lee Enfield ·303 rifle and ten blank rounds of ammunition. Fortunately we had no trouble with terrorists.' Tony Perrett also remembers the beaches of Cyprus well: 'We enjoyed some relaxing banyans on the beaches of "Golden Sands" leave camp near Famagusta. The nearest I got to any action on the island was whilst on a trip to a concert party at an Army camp. Strict security was in force and after I was safely back on board the *Eagle* I

learned that a bomb had exploded in the camp's boiler house shortly after we had left. I actually celebrated my 29th birthday at the "Golden Sands" leave camp.'

Although most members of the ship's company vividly remember the beaches of Cyprus, the *Eagle* was actually at short notice for operations and placed on a war footing. This affected all departments, but in particular the *Eagle's* diving teams who were up well before sunrise while the ship was at anchor in order to search the underwater hull, and they were also detailed to the destroyers and frigates that did not carry their own diving teams. Whilst at sea there were round-the-clock flying programmes and during any breaks from these operations the gun control and supply teams were exercised, which meant that the noise of the aircraft was replaced by the almost non-stop firing of the ship's main defensive armament. Meanwhile, throughout all this the engine room department continued their efforts, under hot and trying conditions, to repair the defective evaporators. As if this was not enough, in late June the ship began regular replenishments of stores from RFA *Retainer*, which proved to be more efficient than storing whilst in harbour and more popular. There was excitement of a different sort one morning when, out of the blue, five unknown minesweepers appeared. In

The *Eagle* at anchor in the Bosphorus during her visit to Istanbul.   *(M. Pack)*

response to *Eagle's* request for an exchange of identities, the strangers replied: 'You can tell our nationality from our flag.' However, as they were flying the ensign of the recently formed United Arab Republic, it was clear that they were not going to follow normal courtesies.

Finally, on Wednesday 2 July, the *Eagle* left her patrol area off Cyprus to return to Malta for a self-maintenance period, and after launching the squadrons to Hal Far she steamed into Grand Harbour to berth alongside Parlatorio Wharf on the afternoon of 4 July. However, the news on the morning of 14 July, that King Faisal of Iraq, his son and the country's Premier had been overthrown in a military coup led by General Kassim, led to *Eagle's* 48 hours' notice for steam being reduced to immediate notice. The coup in Iraq was followed by a request from Lebanon and Jordan for military help from the USA and Britain, and the *Eagle*, as Britain's major naval unit in the Mediterranean, was ordered to sea. After a great deal of hard work by everyone the *Eagle* left Grand Harbour on the morning of Wednesday 16 July, and during the afternoon she embarked her aircraft before steaming east at high speed. The efforts of the ship's company were recognized in a signal from the C-in-C Mediterranean:

'The First Sea Lord congratulates *Eagle* and Malta Dockyard on getting the ship away so unexpectedly early, and so do I.'

Over the next few days the political situation in the Middle East remained somewhat confused, with news of Iraqi army units advancing to Baghdad to fight the rebels while other reports stated that the rebels were in firm control. What had become clear was the fact that King Faisal and his son, and General Nuri, the Premier, had been murdered. The *Eagle* was ordered to an area south of Cyprus to assist in providing support for King Hussein of Jordan who was, in fact, a cousin of ex-King Faisal and a partner in the Arab Federation. Soon after leaving Malta there had been a small fire in lagging in *Eagle's* Y boiler room, but this had been quickly extinguished. However, just 24 hours later, at 1.30pm on Thursday 17 July, there was a much more serious fire in Y boiler room which caused the internal brickwork of a boiler furnace to collapse and also left the back plating burned away. Fortunately, further damage was prevented by shutting down the boiler and reducing the revs on Y engine room, but next morning it was decided to isolate both Y boiler and engine rooms and to disconnect Y engine room shaft. Even more serious

'Goofers' watching flying operations in the Mediterranean. *(A. J. Perrett)*

was the news that other boilers might also go the same way and the situation called for a lot of hard work by the engineering department to repair the damage and to carefully nurse the other boilers.

Early in the evening of Friday 18 July, 802 Sea Hawk Squadron were embarked after a 36-hour, six-stage flight from the UK. The same day *Eagle* was joined by her escorts and these included HM Ships *Cavendish*, *Dunkirk*, *Salisbury* and *Torquay*. By 10.30pm that evening, after refuelling, the force was stationed off the coast of Israel, about 50 miles from Haifa, and the first operational details - to cover the airlift to Amman - were launched. For the next five days the *Eagle's* squadrons provided round-the-clock air cover, codenamed 'Operation Fortitude', and by Wednesday 23 July the airlift to Jordan was completed. However, in the early hours of that day there was a tragic accident on board *Eagle* when, at 3.04am, a fully armed Sea Venom of 894 Squadron with two aircrew crashed into the stern round-down whilst attempting to land. The resulting explosion killed both the pilot, Lt A. G. Harman RN, and the observer, Sub-Lt A. J. Hayward RN, and later that morning, a funeral service was held for them on the quarterdeck.

The completion of 'Operation Fortitude' on 23 July provided a welcome break while the force refuelled. That evening flying operations resumed as the *Eagle's* squadrons covered the withdrawal of the naval force to the Cyprus area and the next day, at just after 11am, the *Eagle* anchored off Famagusta Harbour. During the five days of the operation *Eagle* had flown 500 sorties, 250 of which had been covering missions for air transports, 136 were combat missions and 78 were reconnaissance missions and anti-submarine patrols. In addition the aircraft had flown 34 courier flights, and due to fine work by the ship's Direction teams 208 aircraft were closed and identified. The breakdown of the latter figure was as follows: 121 Allied transport aircraft, 14 UAR civil and seven UAR military aircraft, seven Israeli military aircraft and 59 miscellaneous civil aircraft.

On *Eagle's* return to Famagusta the ship's company renewed their friendship with the local army units who opened their canteen facilities. In return many of the military personnel and their families were invited on board whenever weather and curfew conditions permitted. However, on the morning of Wednesday 30 July the *Eagle* weighed anchor and put to sea once again to resume its operational duties off the coast of Cyprus. The next four weeks were taken up with intensive flying operations, broken only by short spells at anchor off Akrotiri or Famagusta. During this period the ship took part in exercises with the US Navy's carriers *Saratoga* and *Essex*, and she was joined by HMS *Albion* which had been dispatched from the UK with Army reinforcements for Malta. Fortunately, the *Albion* was also able to relieve *Eagle*

for duties off Cyprus and on Friday 22 August FOAC transferred his flag to *Albion* and the *Eagle* left the area for Malta. Next day the C-in-C Mediterranean, Admiral Sir Charles Lambe, embarked by helicopter for a tour of the ship and to congratulate everyone on board for their efforts throughout the weeks of political tension in the region. Later that morning the *Eagle* secured alongside Parlatorio Wharf in Grand Harbour.

During the *Eagle's* stay in Malta the ship's engineers and dockyard staff worked to repair the boiler brickwork, but it was also a time for relaxation and Tony Perrett, together with three chums, hired a small car in order to tour Malta and the neighbouring island of Gozo. When *Eagle* put to sea once again on 9 September 1958, she had embarked a party of senior officers and, more popularly, a group of Wrens. Apparently there was a greater rush of volunteers to entertain the latter group than there was for the former, but all enjoyed watching the squadrons returning from Hal Far. Later that day, after disembarking all the visitors, the *Eagle* set course for Cyprus where she was to relieve the *Albion* and resume support duties for the Army units operating against EOKA terrorists.

For the remainder of September the *Eagle* operated off Cyprus and it was 3 October before she returned to Malta, having been relieved by the *Bulwark* which was returning from the Far East Station, and the ship's company were at last able to prepare for the much delayed visit to Istanbul. The passage back to Malta was enlivened by the arrival on board of two owls who took up residence in the PTI's store and, being fed a diet of prime beef, they were in no hurry to leave. On *Eagle's* last day in Grand Harbour the newly modernized HMS *Victorious* entered the port. This was their first meeting, but in 1941 the *Victorious* had met *Eagle's* ill-fated predecessor. At 10.15am next morning, Tuesday 14 October, the *Eagle* in company with the cruiser *Sheffield*, which was flying the flag of C-in-C Mediterranean, left Malta for the Dardanelles and the city of Istanbul. Their arrival three days later was marred by high winds and rain and the ship's company remained at anchor watches for most of the day. Fortunately, by next morning the weather had improved and leave was granted. Tony Perrett gives a vivid description of his activities during the visit: 'This was a very interesting run ashore and I took the ferry over to Uskador on the Asian side and saw the Scutari Hospital where Florence Nightingale had served during the Crimean campaign. I then took another ferry up the Bosphorus to Sariyer and returned to the ship by bus later that day. Many of the ship's company took it upon themselves to visit the "red light" district in Genel-ev-Street, which was known to most matelots as "Two and a half Street", to see the "ladies" sitting in their windows of each house. Most, like me, only went to view the spectacle, but some ventured in. I remember buying some Turkish Delight in Istanbul to bring home as gifts, but by the time

During November 1958 the *Eagle* was dry docked at Gibraltar. Here she is shown in No 1 dry dock at the colony's Naval Dockyard.
(M. Pack)

we reached Devonport it was crawling with maggots. A lot of people who had bought sheepskin coats found them to be similarly infested. Before we left Istanbul on 23 October the Royal Marines Beat Retreat in Taxim Square, which was very popular and drew large crowds.'

After leaving Istanbul the *Eagle* returned to the Cyprus area and the *Bulwark* was able to depart westwards for home, for paying off and conversion to a commando ship. On 29 October Lieutenants Robinson, Forbes and Readings, in a Skyraider of 849A Flight, made the 10,000th deck landing of the commission, which was quite an achievement in just 15 months and the event was celebrated with a bottle of 'bubbly' by Vice-Admiral Bingley, Captain Frewen and the aircrew. It was decided to dry dock the *Eagle* at Gibraltar in early November for repairs to a worn A bracket and so, on the last day of October, the ship's air group, apart from 802 Squadron which flew home, was launched to Hal Far. Next day *Eagle* moored in Grand Harbour for just long enough to disembark the squadron personnel, before she sailed west for Gibraltar where she was installed in the Dockyard's No 1 dry dock for 13 days. In

fact this was the only dry dock in the Mediterranean large enough to accommodate the *Eagle* and, even so, there were only inches to spare on either side.

After leaving Gibraltar on 17 November the *Eagle* returned to Malta where the squadrons were re-embarked and the ship spent six days cross-operating with the *Victorious*. On Friday 28 November, much to the relief of everyone on board the *Eagle*, courses were set westwards for Gibraltar with the prospect of returning to the UK for Christmas. After a very brief stop in Gibraltar Bay the *Eagle* steamed out into the Atlantic and turned north for home. Tony Perrett remembers the last few days: 'All the aircraft were flown off to shore establishments on 2 December and that same evening we ground crews put on an evening concert party, with the guest of honour Rear-Admiral Charles Evans, who was to take over as FOAC and who had flown on board for the last night of the commission. Next day we steamed up the Hamoaze and secured alongside. It was a great relief to be home for Christmas as there were times when we had wondered whether we would make it.

In January 1959 the *Eagle* made a five-day visit to Naples. This view shows her anchored in the harbour. *(A. J. Perrett)*

With Christmas and the New Year leave periods over, the ship's company prepared for the final deployment of the commission which, once again, would take the *Eagle* to the Mediterranean Station. On Tuesday 13 January 1959 Rear-Admiral C. L. G. Evans CB CBE DSO DSC took up his appointment as FOAC, and embarked in the *Eagle*. Admiral Bingley left the ship to take up his appointment as C-in-C Mediterranean while his flag was struck, and that of Rear-Admiral Evans was hoisted. Admiral Bingley's car was towed from the ship by his staff and the Heads of Department, which was quite an achievement because the

Admiral's driver forgot to release the handbrake. That evening a signal from Admiral Bingley was received on board, which sums up the team spirit of *Eagle's* ship's company. It read: 'Goodbye and good luck to the best and most friendly flagship I have ever met.'

Next morning, at 7.30am, the *Eagle* left her berth and steamed down the Hamoaze once again and, despite the inclement weather conditions, she embarked the air group. After another day's flying exercises had been successfully completed, Captain Frewen was able to announce that the climax of the commission, just before the *Eagle* paid off in

April, would be a visit from Her Majesty The Queen who would be visiting her 'special' ship for the last time before the modernization programme. Later that evening the *Eagle* set courses for Gibraltar and the Mediterranean Fleet.

After spending two days in Gibraltar the *Eagle* steamed into the Mediterranean, in time to take part in 'Exercise Janex' in which her main task was to launch air strikes on the cruiser *Bermuda* and her escorts. In just a few hours the *Eagle* showed what she was capable of by launching almost 100 sorties. Hardly had this exercise finished than she joined the next one, an air defence exercise with the Italian Navy and Air Force in the Gulf of Taranto, code-named 'Exercise Britadex'. This time the weather was distinctly Arctic, with cold northerly gales and frequent squally showers of snow or hail which, at times, grounded all the aircraft. During the exercise the UHF D/F developed faults and the tasks of the REA and RO, who had to carry out running repairs, were far from enviable. However, on Thursday 29 January to everyone's relief, the *Eagle* entered Naples for a five-day visit. During the stay trips were laid on to Capri, Sorrento and to Rome where 84 members of the ship's company had the privilege of an audience with the Pope. However, for many, the main preoccupation was the exchange rate and the local wine.

The *Eagle* left Naples on Tuesday 3 February to take part in 'Exercise Febex' with HMS *Centaur* and the Dartmouth Training Squadron. Once again the severe weather made operations very uncomfortable and on Saturday 7 February *Eagle* entered Grand Harbour for a self-maintenance period. For the ship's company this stay in Malta was enlivened by the carnival parades and firework displays in Valletta. However, the stay was almost cut short when, on the morning of 18 February, gale force winds which are known locally as 'gregales', blew up without warning. At one stage the *Eagle* was at her very exposed mooring in Bighi Bay and two hours away from having steam on her main engines, with winds registering 45 knots. Tugs were sent to stand by in case her moorings broke, but the weather was so severe that they were unable to take the strain of the carrier. The ship was flooded down, so that if she did break adrift she would ground at maximum draught. In addition, all serviceable aircraft were ranged on the flight deck as the ship's only source of power in case the worst should happen. Fortunately, the mooring ropes held and by the early afternoon there was steam on the main engines and the winds were moderating. Next day the weather delayed the ship's sailing for 24 hours, so when the *Eagle* left Grand Harbour on the morning of Friday 20 February there was only half a day left for joint exercises with the *Centaur*.

During the forenoon of 21 February the *Eagle's* port catapult was badly damaged when the towing hook of a Sea Hawk broke during its launch. The catapult, which was suddenly released from its load, carried on through and punched away large sections of plating from the round-down. Although the Sea Hawk was damaged, the pilot, Lt B. Brown RN, was able to land his aircraft safely, but the oldest catapult in the Navy, which had made 15,085 launches, was completely unserviceable. After anchoring for a few hours at Marsaxlokk on 22 February, the *Eagle* left the area for the western Mediterranean where she rendezvoused with the *Victorious* for flying operations off Gibraltar. During this period, on the last day of February, Lt Grier-Rees, in a Sea Hawk of 806 Squadron, gave a practical demonstration of the use of the nylon crash barrier when he was unable to lower his landing hook. It happened at about 10.30am when Lt Grier-Rees, coming into the circuit, found he could not operate his dive brakes. It did not take him long to find out that he had a complete hydraulic failure. He carried out his emergency drill and managed to lower his undercarriage, but his hook remained up. The first impression he got as he came in to land and saw the crash barrier was, 'Gosh! That flimsy thing won't hold me.' His second thought, when he hit it was, 'I've gone right through!' However, all was well. He was surprised by the gentleness of the arresting action before the barrier brought him to a standstill at the end of its stretch. He then found himself going backwards, but by quickly applying his brakes he came to a halt at a slight angle across the flight deck. Fortunately, the pilot was unhurt and not a great deal of damage was done to his aircraft.

On 2 March 1959 the Governor of Gibraltar, General Sir Charles Keightley, who had visited the ship in 1956 after 'Operation Musketeer', embarked by Gannet to watch a flying display before the *Eagle* entered harbour and moored alongside Gibraltar's South Mole. After a ten-day visit, during which the ship's various sporting teams won a number of fleet trophies, a children's party was organized and the *Eagle* herself was opened to visitors, she sailed on Friday 13 March to anchor in Gibraltar Bay and to transfer most of the Venom squadron by lighter to the *Victorious*. In return the *Victorious* parted with her flight of Skyraiders and helicopters. In the meantime repairs continued on the port catapult and the *Eagle* was finally able to sail at 1pm on 15 March to take part in 'Exercise Dawn Breeze'. During the exercise FOAC transferred his flag to *Victorious*, while *Eagle* flew the flag of Admiral Sir William Davis KCB DSO, the C-in-C Home Fleet.

The exercise took the form of a run-in to the south-west coast of England to launch strikes on airfields in Cornwall against the opposition of RAF Bomber Command. As the port catapult was serviceable once again the Venom squadron returned 'home' from the *Victorious*, changing place with the Skyraiders. During the afternoon a helicopter from the ship's flight transferred all the squadron personnel, moving 109 passengers and 7,000lb of stores in just over two hours. Unfortunately, on the last day of the

Top: Mount Vesuvius, as seen from the *Eagle's* flight deck.

(*A. J. Perrett*)

Middle: The *Eagle* anchored in Weymouth Bay shortly before the Queen's visit in April 1959.

(*A. J. Perrett*)

Bottom: Looking very smart, the *Eagle* awaits the visit of her royal sponsor, Her Majesty Queen Elizabeth II, before paying off and undergoing reconstruction in Devonport Dockyard.

(*A. J. Perrett*)

The *Eagle* alongside 5 & 6 wharves of Devonport Dockyard in May 1959. Six months later she was taken over by the dockyard for a major modernization programme.

(Maritime Photo Library)

exercise the port catapult finally gave up altogether and the next day goofers were treated to the unusual spectacle of the Sea Hawk squadron making free take-offs using the full length of the flight deck. Finally, during the afternoon of Monday 23 March, the *Eagle* moored at C buoy in Plymouth Sound and 24 hours later she steamed up-harbour to secure alongside 6 & 7 berths.

Following the Easter leave periods for both watches, Monday 13 April 1959 was to be rather an unusual, but special, day for the *Eagle*. 'Call The Hands' took place at the early hour of 5.30am and then at 6.30am 400 wives and children embarked for a 'Families Day' at sea. At 7.45am, when the *Eagle* steamed down the Hamoaze, the usual immaculate 'Procedure Alpha' was replaced by almost 100 children. It was said that after the *Eagle* passed the breakwater of Plymouth Sound there was an unusually high demand for seasickness tablets from the sick bay. Although the idea of a 'Families Day' was not new, having been tried in both the *Ark Royal* and the *Bulwark*, this was the first time that relatives had been able to watch the full flying routine aboard an aircraft carrier. Nearly a quarter of the visitors were children who clambered about and roamed around Britain's biggest warship. The idea of such a day, with a full-scale flying programme, had been urged repeatedly by the ship's company and approval had come within weeks of the ship paying off. A staunch supporter of the idea had been Rear-Admiral Evans, who rightly believed that it provided a great incentive for recruiting. As he said at the time: 'No one sees a carrier performing her

proper role when visiting her in harbour and I have told other commanding officers that I would like to see them adopting similar plans.' The visitors saw flying displays by Sea Hawks, Sea Venoms, Gannets and Skyraiders, and afterwards they watched a film of the *Eagle's* activities which had been made earlier in the commission. Following this they toured the ship, taking the route which the Queen would use during her forthcoming visit. After some six hours at sea the guests disembarked into tenders in Plymouth Sound and shortly afterwards the *Eagle* sailed for Brest to take part in celebrations marking the tenth anniversary of NATO.

After battling through the worst gale of the commission the *Eagle* entered the French port at 11am on Wednesday 15 April and berthed between the battleship *Richelieu* and the new French aircraft carrier *Clemenceau*. As she entered harbour strong winds were still blowing, and while she manoeuvred alongside her berth the engines of the aircraft on the flight deck were started to help swing the bows into place. Later Admiral Evans made a speech in French regarding the new French vessel, which, given the demise of British carrier aviation, sounds ironic today: 'The building of the *Clemenceau*, in addition to the carrier which you already have, as well as the development of new naval aircraft, is evidence that the French Navy has the same view of the importance of carrier-borne air support as the Royal Navy.' During her stay in Brest the *Eagle* was opened to visitors and a party for 400 children was held. In the event it was estimated that over 1,000 turned up, many of whom were suspected of being over 18 years of age but, as always, the Navy coped with the situation in its usual efficient style and the children, who were from schools and orphanages in the Brest area, enjoyed themselves for over two hours with roundabouts, swings and aerial flights as well as the usual sideshows. Afterwards the ship's company, dressed as pirates, served tea in the lower hangar.

The *Eagle* left Brest at 2pm on Tuesday 21 April 1959, to steam up the Channel to Weymouth Bay where she anchored the following evening to prepare for the grand finale of the commission. The visit to the ship by Her Majesty The Queen, which Captain Frewen had announced in January, had been set for Wednesday 29 April and for the next week the ship's company would rehearse the flying exercises which had been planned for the occasion.

During the week preceding the visit the weather on the south coast was particularly unsettled and at one stage the whole event was in danger of being cancelled. When 29 April dawned cloudy with the threat of rain it did not look too promising, but *Eagle's* luck held and from time to time the sun even shone. The Queen arrived at Weymouth Railway Station, accompanied by Prince Charles, at exactly 10am and from there they were driven to Weymouth Harbour to board the Royal Barge for the short journey into Weymouth Bay. As the barge approached the *Eagle* a 21-gun royal salute reverberated around the bay and at 10.25am the Queen and Prince Charles embarked in the carrier which then weighed anchor and put to sea. By Her Majesty's own wish the keynote of the visit was informality, and while the *Eagle* steamed out to her exercise area, the Queen and Prince Charles made a strenuous tour of the mess decks and accommodation, in the course of which they met and spoke with 150 officers and men. It was a happy, light-hearted tour, which soon showed how well the Queen knew the ship and how closely she had watched the progress of the *Eagle's* career. During the tour Prince Charles made visits of his own to an engine room and to one of the 4-inch gun turrets and to the hangars. By the time the tour was completed the *Eagle* was well out to sea

and the visitors were able to witness a mass take-off of 33 aircraft for a flying display, the climax of which was a fly-past of 24 Sea Venoms and Sea Hawks.

After lunch the Queen took the salute at a march past of the ship's company and following this the two youngest members presented gifts on behalf of everyone on board. For the Queen and the Duke of Edinburgh there were two silver rosebowls for use in the Royal Yacht, Prince Charles was given a miniature rum tub adapted as a stud box, and Princess Anne's gift was a gold bracelet bearing the ship's crest. The visit was a huge success and every one of the 2,350 members of the ship's company had an opportunity of seeing the visitors at close quarters.

At 1.30pm that day the *Eagle* anchored in Weymouth Bay once again and just over an hour later the Queen and Prince Charles disembarked. The visit had been a complete success and it was the first time that a reigning British monarch had made a journey from London just to visit one warship. As the *Eagle*, with her paying-off pennant flying, weighed anchor and set course for Devonport, the following signal was received from Her Majesty: 'I greatly enjoyed visiting *Eagle* with my son, the Prince of Wales, at the end of what has been a happy and highly successful commission. I was much impressed by the fine bearing of *Eagle's* ship's company and by the high standard of the flying. I was also pleased to see the smart appearance of the escorting ships and those which I passed this morning. Please convey my congratulations to all officers and ratings under your command. Splice the Main Brace!'

At 5pm that afternoon the *Eagle's* squadrons were ranged for take-off for the last time in the commission, and then flown off safely to their air stations. Next morning, at 11am, the carrier passed through the breakwater of Plymouth Sound and made a ceremonial entry into Devonport Dockyard, where she was secured alongside 5 & 6 wharves at just before 1pm. A week later over one fifth of the ship's company left the *Eagle* and the process of paying off continued until November 1959 when she was taken over by the dockyard for a modernization refit which would last for over four years.

Following her modernization the *Eagle* left Plymouth for her sea trials on Tuesday 19 May 1964. In this view she steams past Mount Wise and Admiralty House for Plymouth Sound and the open sea.

(Mrs K. M. Strickland)

Chapter Nine

Fourth Commission - A New Silhouette

Originally the *Eagle's* modernization refit had been scheduled to last for three years at an estimated cost of £20 million. However, it soon became clear that the work would take four years, with a substantial increase in expenditure to £30 million. There were some, including senior officers, who criticized the policy of modernizing older vessels, and particularly the *Eagle*, because of the obvious limitations imposed in fitting so much new equipment into an existing hull. However, considering the fact that a new aircraft carrier would, even in the early 1960s, have cost at least £60 million, the modernization of the *Eagle* was defended by the First Lord of the Admiralty, Lord Carrington. He pointed out to Parliament in early 1961 that during the *Eagle's* refit full use would be made of the latest techniques in automation, and the developments incorporated would prolong the life of the ship and enable it to operate the most up-to-date naval aircraft and weapons systems.

And so the *Eagle* underwent a complete transformation. She was installed with a fully angled flight deck of $8\frac{1}{2}°$, and the island superstructure was completely rebuilt so that it was half as long again as the original design. Much of this alteration was caused by the need to fit the new Type 984 radar with its large 'searchlight' scanner which occupied the forward position on the island superstructure. In the after position was the Type 963 radar which was for controlling aircraft in blind-approach landings. The 4-inch armour on the flight deck had to be removed and replaced by $1\frac{1}{2}$-inch armour and the void space was filled with polyurethane foam, which was its first use in a naval dockyard.

The four forward 4.5-inch gun turrets were removed and the entire light anti-aircraft battery was replaced by six Seacat short-range missile launchers (three to starboard, two to port and one right aft). The *Eagle's* two hydraulic catapults were replaced by new steam catapults which had added punch. The 'waist' catapult on the angled deck had an extra-long stroke (199ft) and was capable of launching aircraft loaded to capacity in reduced wind conditions. It was also the largest to be fitted to any aircraft carrier in a European Navy. The forward catapult, on the port side of the flight deck, was 151ft long and could easily launch the latest heavy naval aircraft. The aircraft parking area was further enlarged by another extension forward of the island on the starboard side and by the removal of the starboard catapult. As well as improvements to equipment, the accommodation for the ship's company was also modified, with the wardroom being moved up two decks to the level of the quarterdeck and with bunks being fitted to all mess

decks, in place of hammocks. Further comfort was added by the provision of full air-conditioning in all the accommodation areas and many of the working spaces. She was, in fact, the first RN ship to be fully air-conditioned and this gave rise to a host of design and technical problems because experience with such large projects was very limited at that time. New galleys with the most modern equipment offered a full cafeteria service and multi-choice messing, whilst a NAAFI canteen, a bar, soda fountain, ice cream counter and barber's shop were included among the ship's amenities. However, the need for extra workshop space meant that the after section of the lower hangar was lost, resulting in a reduction of aircraft stowage. This factor, combined with the heavier aircraft, meant that *Eagle's* complement was reduced to 36 fixed-wing and ten rotary-wing aircraft, half as many as she had originally been designed to carry. To all outward observers, however, the most noticeable change in the ship's silhouette was the addition of the large, dustbin-like 984 radar scanner on the island superstructure, which was the principal outward sign of a mass of electronic gadgetry and automation.

By the winter of 1963 a number of key appointments, including her commanding officer, Captain L. D. Empson RN, had been made and in the New Year of 1964 the *Eagle* was afloat once more and alongside 5 & 6 wharves in the dockyard. Captain Empson had joined the Royal Navy in 1940 as a Naval Airman Second Class, but he was quickly commissioned as a Sub-Lieutenant (A) RNVR and soon qualified as a pilot. He had, in fact, served with 812 Squadron in the previous HMS *Eagle* and in 1944 he was permanently commissioned into the Royal Navy. Nearly all of Captain Empson's career had been concerned with naval aviation and his appointment to command the *Eagle* was the first occasion on which an ex-RNVR officer had become the captain of an aircraft carrier.

The second chapter of *Eagle's* career began at 9am on Thursday 16 January 1964, when the White Ensign was hoisted on commissioning for dockyard sea trials. That afternoon Captain Empson addressed the ship's company and the following day the C-in-C Plymouth, Admiral Sir Nigel Henderson KCB OBE, toured the ship. Finally, at 2pm on Saturday 25 January, the *Eagle* slipped her moorings and, under her own power, steamed out to Plymouth Sound and moored at C buoy. It was the first time she had left the shelter of Devonport Dockyard for four years and nine months.

Over the next 12 days the *Eagle* carried out trials in Lyme Bay, and of particular interest were the machinery

The *Eagle* passes between Hoe Pier and Drake's Island on her passage through Plymouth Sound for sea trials. Her type 984 radar, with its large 'searchlight' scanner, and the new *Seacat* missile launcher can be seen where her port forward 4·5-inch guns used to be.

(Mrs K. M. Stickland)

Naval sea power in the early 1960s. HMS *Eagle* in Plymouth Sound. *(Mrs K. M. Strickland)*

The *Eagle* at sea once again. Here she has just passed the breakwater of Plymouth Sound close to HMS *Kent*.

(*Mrs K. M. Stickland*)

trials. Although the *Eagle's* conventional steam propulsion remained intact, a system for the remote control of both the main boilers and main engines had been added so that it was possible to control the whole of the main propulsion machinery from a central machinery control room. The ship was also steered by means of a new type of steering console which allowed 'power steering', and employed a small joystick in place of the conventional ship's wheel. During the morning of Thursday 30 January one of the *Eagle's* former commanding officers, Vice-Admiral Sir Michael Le Fanu, who was now the Third Sea Lord, visited the ship in company with a government minister. The initial trials ended on the morning of Thursday 6 February when the *Eagle* was secured alongside 5 & 6 wharves in Devonport Dockyard and was once again taken over by the dockyard authorities.

The *Eagle's* first commission following her modernization started in earnest in early May 1964, when the majority of her ship's company joined the ship. The commissioning ceremony took place on Thursday 14 May and at 8am that morning Colours were hoisted. At 11am the official guests started to arrive and they included the mayors of both Plymouth and Exeter and the Flag Officer Naval Air Command, Vice-Admiral R. M. Smeeton. The principal guests were Admiral Sir Nigel Henderson and Lady Henderson, who cut the commissioning cake. Next morning the Admiral Superintendent's final inspection took place and in the afternoon the ship was opened to relatives

of the ship's company, attracting 1,700 families in the space of a few hours. It was at just after midday on Tuesday 19 May 1964 when the *Eagle* put to sea once again to start her official trials and work-up, and within hours of her leaving Plymouth Sound the inevitable Soviet trawler was on hand to investigate and, no doubt, report her movements. The remainder of May was spent in the Channel undergoing machinery trials and then the *Eagle* returned to Devonport Dockyard where defects were rectified while she lay alongside for the first two weeks of June.

It was Friday 19 June 1964 when, with full ceremony, the *Eagle* left Devonport once again, and next day the first fixed-wing aircraft, those famous and well-loved aeroplanes from the 1930s, De Havilland Tiger Moths, made deck landings. However, this 100mph biplane was a far cry from the carrier's squadrons which would shortly be joining. What the Soviet trawlers thought of flying operations that day is not recorded. Towards the end of June Seacat missile firings were carried out in Cardigan Bay and speed trials were undertaken in the Firth of Clyde, off Arran. On the last day of June the *Eagle* set course back to Devonport for two more weeks alongside in the dockyard. This time the ground crews of 800 Buccaneer, 899 Sea Vixen, 800B Scimitar and 849D Gannet Squadrons joined the ship, as preparations were made for the carrier's flying trials. *Eagle* put to sea once again on Monday 13 July 1964 and the following day, in Lyme Bay, 'Flying Stations' was

By the autumn of 1964 the *Eagle's* squadrons had joined her and in this view six Buccaneers of 800 Squadron, nine Sea Vixens of 899 Squadron and four Wessex helicopters of 820 Squadron are arranged on the flight deck. *(A. Moore)*

In January 1965 the *Eagle* arrived at Singapore for the first time in her career. Here she is shown in the Johore Strait on her way to the Naval Base on the island's north coast. *(Fleet Air Arm Museum)*

'Crossing the Line' 8 January 1965. King Neptune embarks. *(A. Moore)*

intervention saved their lives and, after righting their dinghy, they were taken ashore shaken but unhurt.

The flying trials started on the first day of September, and three days later the *Eagle* made an 18-day visit to Portsmouth where she berthed at Middle Slip Jetty. She left for Lyme Bay once again on Tuesday 22 September and flying trials were resumed. During the period of the trials she was visited by the First Sea Lord, Admiral Sir David Luce, and by a government minister. The programme ended on the last day of September and the following afternoon the *Eagle* began her first foreign visit following her return to service when she secured alongside the Quai d' Armament at Brest, five and a half years after the last foreign visit of her third commission. This time, however, it was a fleeting 48-hour stopover and during the afternoon of Saturday 3 October she sailed for Gibraltar. After six days of exercises the *Eagle* secured alongside 48 berth in the colony's dockyard, and during the ten-day stay the ship provided a ceremonial guard for a Trafalgar Day parade, and the Governor of Gibraltar took the salute at Divisions on the flight deck. For most of the ship's company, however, there was the attraction of some duty-free shopping and the High Street stores did a brisk trade. The visit ended on Friday 23 October 1964 when the carrier set course for Devonport, through severe gales and very heavy seas which necessitated a reduction in speed in order to avoid damage to the ship.

The *Eagle* returned to the UK on Monday 26 October, and, after being cleared by Customs, she then left Plymouth Sound to carry out flying demonstrations for members of the Press. The first week of November was spent in Lyme Bay completing her work-up before she returned to Devonport, where the ship's company took foreign service leave before the *Eagle* left for six months on the Far East Station. During the period spent in Devonport the *Ark Royal* was commissioned and, after her work-up, she would follow the *Eagle* to the Far East. The *Eagle* was visited by a BBC camera team and the entertainer Val Doonican, who with the singing duo 'The Ladybirds', performed for the ship's company and for TV audiences.

On Tuesday 1 December 1964 the squadron personnel joined the ship and later the same afternoon, flying the flag of FOAC, Rear-Admiral H. R. B. Janvrin CB DSC, *Eagle* left Devonport for Lyme Bay where the air group was embarked before courses were set for the Mediterranean. Early on the morning of Saturday 5 December the ship was stopped and a wreath was laid over the spot where the previous *Eagle* had been sunk on 11 August 1942. Three days later the *Eagle* anchored off Port Said and in the early hours of 12 December she started her southbound transit of the Suez Canal, which she cleared later that same afternoon. Three days after leaving Port Suez, the *Eagle* moored to buoys in Aden Harbour for just long enough to refuel before she sailed for exercises off Aden with the

piped and the Vixens and Gannets of 899 and 849D Squadrons spent a long and arduous day carrying out landings and launches from both catapults. Next day it was the turn of the Buccaneers of 800 Squadron. The flying trials continued for another eight days before the *Eagle* returned to Devonport on 23 July for seasonal leave periods to be taken.

Navy Days at Devonport took place over the first three days of August in 1964 and the *Eagle* was, of course, the star attraction. During the three afternoons that the ship was opened to the public, which amounted to 12 hours in total, *Eagle* attracted 19,000 visitors. With over 1,500 people boarding the ship every hour, the problems voiced by Admiral Hughes-Hallett in March 1953 had obviously been overcome. It was the last week in August before the *Eagle* left Devonport again, this time for Portland in order to work up the squadrons. The first weekend was spent at anchor in Weymouth Bay and on the morning of Saturday 29 August the ship's picket boat went to the rescue of a family whose sailing dinghy had capsized. This timely

'Exercise FOTEX 65' in March 1965. Astern of the *Eagle* are HMS *Bulwark*, HMAS *Melbourne* and HMS *Victorious*.

(*A. Moore*)

frigates *Mohawk* and *Whitby*. On Sunday 20 December, after four days of exercises, the *Eagle* anchored briefly off Aden where FOAC disembarked and the carrier then left for Mombasa for a far more hospitable Christmas than Aden could ever hope to offer. During her stay in Kilindini Harbour the woodcarving stalls of Kilindini Road and the beaches of Silversands did good business, as did the safari tours to Tsavo Park. Christmas Eve saw the Royal Marines Band playing for an impromptu carol service on the flight deck at 11pm, and at a carol service the following morning on the quarterdeck. After this the band split up to visit every mess deck on the ship where a 'certain

refreshment' was imbibed at each stop. However, to their disappointment, after playing a selection of carols outside Captain Empson's cabin, they were informed that he wasn't in. To everyone's delight the ship's stay in Mombasa was extended because of generator trouble which necessitated spare parts being flown out from the UK.

The 11-day stay at Mombasa finally ended on the afternoon of 4 January 1965, when the *Eagle* sailed for Singapore in company with the *Whitby*. The 'Crossing the Line' ceremony was held on Friday 8 January when, on a hot, sunny morning, Captain Empson met King Neptune on the flight deck to welcome him and his court on board

Four carriers in the South China Sea. Astern of the *Eagle* are the *Bulwark*, HMAS *Melbourne*, and in the distance, the *Victorious*. (*A. Moore*)

for several hours of very wet skylarking, which culminated in a battle royal between various groups armed with firemain hoses. On Monday 11 January, during the voyage to Singapore, came the SAR helicopter's first opportunity to carry out a mission of mercy when a seaman suffering from appendicitis was evacuated from the oil tanker MV *World Progress* and brought back to the *Eagle* where the surgeon carried out a successful operation. Two days later the Vixens were launched to RAF Tengah, the Buccaneers to RAF Changi and the Gannets to RAF Seletar, and early the same evening the *Eagle* berthed alongside in Singapore's Naval Base for a 13-day self-maintenance period. During the stay the C-in-C Far East Station, Admiral Sir Desmond Dreyer, visited the ship and addressed the ship's company.

On leaving Singapore in the last week of February the *Eagle* took part in anti-submarine exercises in the area, with HMS *Andrew* providing its services for the pilots of 820 Squadron to practise on. At this time 820 Squadron got another chance to show off their capabilities when the SAR helicopter recovered a man who had fallen overboard. The exercises were broken off for a visit to Subic Bay and the dubious pleasures of Olongapo, which proved to be a real eye-opener for those who were east of Suez for the first time. However, on 23 February, with joint fleet exercises completed, the *Eagle* anchored in Victoria Harbour, Hong Kong, for the ever popular run ashore. As always, the Royal Marines Band was in demand and their concert outside the Town Hall in Victoria was well attended, and two squadron dinners were held, one on a ferryboat and the other in the China Fleet Club.

On leaving Hong Kong during the morning of Thursday 11 March, with HMAS *Derwent*, the *Eagle* returned to the Singapore area where FOAC hoisted his flag once again and 'Exercise Fotex 65' got under way off the west coast of Malaya. The exercise was made bearable by banyans to the island of Pulau Lankowi, now an expensive 1990s holiday resort. Also involved in the exercise were the *Victorious*, the *Bulwark* and the Australian carrier HMAS *Melbourne*. Unfortunately, towards the end of the exercise, at 8.30am on Wednesday 24 March, tragedy struck when a Wessex helicopter of 820 Squadron ditched off *Eagle's* port beam. Despite prompt rescue efforts two of the crew members, Sub-Lt D. F. Clay RN and LEM N. K. Little, were killed and a third crew member, NA Renshaw, was injured. The accident overshadowed a visit to the ship by the C-in-C FES, and it was early evening before operations to recover the wrecked helicopter, which was lying in 30 fathoms of water, were called off. Next day, whilst rehearsing for 'Exercise Showpiece', which was being staged for Malaysian government officials, another of 820 Squadron's Wessex helicopters ditched, but fortunately on this occasion both the crew and the helicopter were rescued safely. Nevertheless, all Wessex flying was suspended until essential modifications had been completed. That afternoon the

funeral service was held for Sub-Lt Clay and LEM Little.

At 10.30am on the morning of Saturday 27 March 1965, the Prime Minister of Malaysia, Tungku Abdul Rahman, together with ministers and defence officials, embarked by helicopter and within an hour the flying display by the Buccaneers of 800 Squadron was under way. Fortunately the event passed off without a hitch and after lunching with FO2 FES, Rear-Admiral Hill-Norton, the Malaysian Prime Minister and his officials left the ship and that evening the *Eagle* moored to B buoy at Singapore Naval Base.

On 1 April *Eagle* left the Naval Base for five days of flying exercises off Malaya's east coast in the region of Pulau Tioman, before returning to Singapore for a 14-day self-maintenance period. When she left the Naval Base on Tuesday 20 April she was homeward bound with only a 48-hour stopover at Aden, much to the relief of the whole ship's company. As someone on board was heard to say, 'It just had to be visited again to confirm that it was as dry and desolate as it looked.' The short visit bore this out, with the duty-free shopping being the only attraction, although with a terrorist campaign under way the Army had strict security precautions in place.

After leaving Aden the *Eagle* made her northbound transit of the Suez Canal on Wednesday 5 May, courses were set for Beirut, and at just before 10am on 7 May the *Eagle* secured alongside the South Mole of Lebanon's capital city. During the stay there was a visit to the ship by the C-in-C of the Lebanese Army and a number of civic officials. As usual the Royal Marines Band was in demand at dances, a ship's football match and a Beating Retreat Ceremony on the flight deck, all in the space of two days. As well as opening the vessel to visitors, the ship's company laid on a children's party and the *Eagle's* cricket team was able to play a game against a team from the British Consulate. After leaving Beirut the *Eagle* steamed west to Malta where she rendezvoused with HMS *Centaur* whose career as an operational aircraft carrier was drawing to a close. As REM Aubrey Moore recalls, 'She had only three Sea Vixens and one Gannet on board and it was clear that her days were numbered.' After exercising for three days the *Eagle* and *Centaur* berthed in Grand Harbour's Bighi Bay, at 12 and 11 berths respectively. Four days later the two carriers left Malta, the *Centaur* bound for Istanbul and the *Eagle* for a fast passage to Devonport. A short seven-hour stop was made off Gibraltar and on Sunday 23 May 1965, as the *Eagle* was crossing the Bay of Biscay, all the serviceable aircraft were launched for Yeovilton and Lossiemouth. Next morning, off Eddystone, Customs officers were embarked and at 12.40pm the *Eagle* secured alongside 5 & 6 berths at Devonport Dockyard. The first leg of the commission was over and a short refit and a change of command lay ahead.

During the morning of Saturday 27 March 1965 the Prime Minister of Malaysia, Tungku Abdul Rahman, together with ministers and defence officials, embarked for 'Exercise Showpiece'. Here they watch Buccaneers and Sea Vixens being launched. *(A. Moore)*

'Exercise Showpiece'. HMAS *Yarra*, followed by two Battle-class radar pickets, steams past the *Eagle*. *(A. Moore)*

HMS *Eagle* with other units of the Far East Fleet during 'Exercise Showpiece'. *(A. Moore)*

In May 1965 the *Eagle* took part in exercises off Malta with HMS *Centaur.* Here the two carriers are seen together.
(Fleet Air Arm Museum)

HMS *Eagle* at her berth in Grand Harbour on the morning of Saturday 15 May 1965, with the *Centaur* in the background, having just passed through the breakwater.   *(Fleet Air Arm Museum)*

Leaving Malta on the morning of Wednesday 19 May 1965. *(A. Moore)*

A Buccaneer leaves the catapult. *(A. Moore)*

HMS *Eagle* embarks stores. *(A. Moore)*

A splendid aerial view of the *Eagle* during her final years. *(K. Rimmer)*

Chapter Ten

Fourth Commission - Beira Patrol

The first week of July 1965 saw the *Eagle* high and dry in Devonport's No 10 dry dock as she underwent a refit prior to starting the second leg of the commission. On Tuesday 20 July there was a change of command as Captain J. C. Y. Roxburgh DSO DSC RN relieved Captain L. D. Empson, when the latter left for an appointment at the Imperial Defence College. Captain Roxburgh had served in submarines during the Second World War, and he had taken part in operations off Norway, in the Bay of Biscay and in the Mediterranean. Between 1942 and 1945 he had commanded the elderly *H43*, and the more modern submarines *United* and *Tapir*. After the war he had served in the battleship *Vanguard* and had commanded the submarine HMS *Turpin*. Captain Roxburgh had served as the Executive Officer in the light fleet carrier HMS *Triumph* in 1955, and in the following year in HMS *Ark Royal*. After commanding the destroyer *Contest* in the late 1950s, Captain Roxburgh had returned to submarines in the early 1960s when he commanded the 3rd Submarine Squadron and the depot ship HMS *Adamant*. Following this Captain Roxburgh was appointed to the Joint Planning Staff at the Ministry of Defence, before taking command of the *Eagle*.

By the end of July the *Eagle* was back alongside 5 & 6 wharves and preparing for sea once again. It was Tuesday 3 August when the ship steamed down the Hamoaze to Plymouth Sound and out to sea, and it is a day which many relatives of ship's company members will always remember as they had embarked that morning for 'Families Day' and several hours at sea. That same afternoon, after the families had disembarked into tenders in Plymouth Sound, the *Eagle* sailed for sea trials in the Channel and in Lyme Bay. These were successfully completed by 10 August and the ship returned to Devonport to prepare for service on the Far East Station.

Two weeks later, on the afternoon of Tuesday 24 August, as the *Eagle* made ready for sea, General Sir Gerald Lathbury GCB DSO MBE, together with Lady Lathbury and their two miniature dachshunds, embarked for the voyage to Gibraltar where General Lathbury was to take up his appointment as Governor. Unfortunately, the Land Rover which was bringing the General's baggage was delayed and he was anxious to hold back the ship's departure, but owing to the *Eagle's* size and draught it was important that she sailed with the high tide. Happily the Land Rover arrived just in time and the *Eagle* sailed at

A Buccaneer of 800 Squadron is launched from the forward catapult. *(A. Moore)*

A very unusual view of the *Eagle's* upper and lower hangars. *(A. Moore)*

4.05pm, only 20 minutes behind schedule. That evening the C-in-C Home Fleet, Admiral Sir John Frewen, arrived on board in a Gannet of 849D Flight for an overnight visit. At 9pm seven more Gannets flew past in formation before landing on board.

Next day, as the *Eagle* steamed south for Gibraltar, the rest of the squadrons were embarked, including the Buccaneers of 800 Squadron, the Scimitars of 800B Flight, the Wessex helicopters of 820 Squadron which, because of fog, had been unable to embark the previous day whilst the ship was alongside, and the Sea Vixens of 899 Squadron. Flying continued for most of the day with deck landing practice for the new arrivals, and two Members of Parliament arrived by Gannet for a short visit.

On the morning of Saturday 28 August the *Eagle* anchored half a mile off the Gibraltar breakwater and shortly afterwards, after a full ceremonial departure, Sir Gerald and Lady Lathbury left the ship by helicopter to take up residence ashore. At noon the *Eagle* weighed anchor and steamed out to an exercise area in the western approaches to Gibraltar where she undertook two and a half days of intensive flying exercises. Following this the carrier left the area bound for Malta, and during the

afternoon of Wednesday 1 September she was stopped off North Africa, in order to re-engage the port inner propeller shaft following minor engine repairs, when a Soviet Kynda-class guided missile destroyer approached to within one cable. Captain Roxburgh launched a helicopter in order to take some photographs of the Russian vessel which was one of four ships that, in the mid-1960s, represented a new generation of surface warships, being armed with SS-N-3 anti-ship guided missiles. Before getting under way again the *Eagle* signalled by light: 'Hope your pictures are as good as mine', to which the Soviet warship, whose commanding officer obviously had a sense of humour, replied: 'Thank you for the compliment.' Following this the *Eagle* tracked the destroyer on the 993 radar before losing it at 36 miles.

Next day the *Eagle* arrived at the exercise area off Malta for the second phase of the work-up programme and this started shortly afterwards with 'Exercise Quick Draw', a 30-hour anti-submarine exercise with the destroyer HMS *Defender* and the RFA *Tidesurge*. Also taking part in the exercise were units of the US Sixth Fleet, including the nuclear attack submarine USS *Haddo* and the conventionally powered submarine USS *Sea Robin*. Sadly, at 7.16am on the morning of Wednesday 8 September, in a

The *Eagle* in the Indian Ocean during her record-breaking Beira Patrol. *(Fleet Air Arm Museum)*

position Lat 35° - 20'N/Long 14° - 26'E, came the first tragedy of the commission when a Sea Vixen of 899 Squadron, flown by Lt A. P. Rayment RN with the observer Sub-Lt R. Matthews RN, hit its port wing on the deck as it landed, turned over onto its back and plunged into the sea alongside the ship. The SAR helicopter was immediately over the scene and a diver went down, and at the same time the ship was stopped and the seaboat lowered. Despite the fact that the SAR diver followed the aircraft down as it sank, he was unable to rescue the crew and both they and the Sea Vixen were lost. At 7.45pm the *Eagle* had to get under way once again in order to recover the aircraft which had been launched shortly before the crash, and following this the work-up exercises were continued. Next day, at 10.15am, a memorial service was held on the quarterdeck for the lost aircrew. On Monday 13 September, at 1.30pm, the *Eagle* secured to No 11 buoy in Malta's Grand Harbour for a ten-day self-maintenance period.

The *Eagle* left Grand Harbour during the afternoon of Thursday 23 September and set course for the exercise area off Malta. At 10.30pm that evening, as the ship passed over the site of the Sea Vixen accident of 8 September, a wreath was laid in memory of Lt Rayment and Sub-Lt Matthews. Next day the *Eagle* embarked stores from RFA *Reliant* and fuelled from RFA *Tidesurge* and, in company with the frigate HMS *Lowestoft* (Captain J. D. Treacher RN, a future CO of HMS *Eagle*), flying exercises started once again.

Meanwhile, in the British colony of Aden, an urban guerrilla war had been going on since November 1964, when the leading terrorist group in the colony, the National Liberation Front (NLF), had initiated a grenade throwing campaign. The activities of the NLF and its

main rival, the Front for the Liberation of Occupied South Yemen (FLOSY), were well organized and utterly ruthless and by 1965 the future for a continued British presence in the area looked quite bleak. As this terrorist campaign began to suck in more and more of the service units stationed in the colony, it was clear that reinforcements would be required to deal with Egyptian and Yemeni sponsored dissidents who were continually harassing the government forces in the Radfan, about 60 miles north of the Aden state boundary. By September 1965 the army presence in Aden had increased from a single battalion to three full-scale battalions and the RAF were deploying three regiment squadrons for the defence of RAF Khormaksar. Most of the terrorist outrages in the colony were confined to the Crater area, with the densely populated area being ideal for the hit-and-run tactics of the terrorists. This then was the situation in the inhospitable British colony when, on Friday 24 September, Captain Roxburgh received orders to proceed to Aden in company with the *Lowestoft* and the RFAs *Tidesurge* and *Reliant*. In fact the Governor of Aden, Sir Richard Turnbull, was about to dissolve the Aden government and take over its responsibilities in the form of direct rule, and the Flag Officer Middle East Station, Rear-Admiral P. N. Howes, had ordered the four vessels to make a fast passage to the colony so that the helicopters would, if necessary, be ready to carry out internal security duties.

The Suez Canal transit was not without incident. After embarking two Egyptian pilots, the *Eagle* entered the canal at 5.32am under the guidance of the senior of them. A few minutes later, owing to an error by the pilot, the ship developed a huge sheer towards the west bank with her head 12 degrees off course. This was followed by a 24 degree lurch to port towards the east bank and Captain Roxburgh had to step in quickly and take over in order to settle the ship, before turning over to the second pilot who navigated her competently to Lake Timsah, while the senior man remained morosely silent at the rear of the bridge. At Lake Timsah relief pilots took over and with a 35-knot wind abeam, steering through the Bitter Lakes was tricky. While entering the channel at the south end of the lakes the ship developed another sheer, but this time everyone was ready for it and, to Captain Roxburgh's relief, the *Eagle* cleared the Suez Canal at 8.30pm after a 15-hour transit.

Following a fast 23-knot passage down the Red Sea with the *Lowestoft*, the *Eagle* arrived off Aden early on the morning of Friday 1 October and anchored in Aden Bay off Fort Tarshyne. With a general strike imposed and sporadic rioting taking place in the colony over the suspension of the constitution, three of the *Eagle's* helicopters were flown ashore to Khormaksar in order to assist with internal security duties and Captain Roxburgh attended meetings with Rear-Admiral Howes and Lt-General Sir Charles Harrington, the C-in-C Middle East. At 11.15am, following Captain Roxburgh's return to the ship, the *Eagle* weighed anchor and put to sea for day and night flying exercises in the Gulf of Aden. During Friday 8 October Mr J. P. W. Mallilieu, the Under Secretary of State for Defence for the Royal Navy in the Labour Government, visited the ship by helicopter to observe the flying exercises. During the visit he spent half an hour with Captain Roxburgh in his sea cabin on the bridge, after which Captain Roxburgh noted in his diary: 'He was not too sanguine over the future of aircraft carriers in the Navy,

which was depressing as I know ours is the answer and *Eagle* really is beginning to tick. The RAF solution looks as if it may prevail.' Prior to his appointment as the *Eagle's* commanding officer Captain Roxburgh had served in the MoD as the Deputy Director of Joint Plans, and he had been directly involved in opposition to the RAF's efforts to promote their 'island bases' policy at the expense of the Fleet Air Arm's fixed-wing aircraft carriers, so the government minister's pessimism appeared to confirm his worst fears.

The next day proved to be very eventful, with flying exercises getting under way during the forenoon. At just after noon a Buccaneer of 800 Squadron, crewed by Lt-Cdr Chase USN and Lt Markley USN, two exchange officers from the US Navy, developed fuel problems whilst carrying out mock attacks on the ship. The aircraft lost power and the pilot was unable to maintain height, and with the plane both underpowered and overweight owing to the unusable fuel it was carrying, it was unable to land on board or ashore at RAF Khormaksar which was closely surrounded by local housing. The two officers were instructed to put the Buccaneer into neutral flight and eject from 2,000 ft, as close to the ship as they possibly could. This they did successfully and the *Eagle's* SAR helicopter had picked them up and returned them on board before their plane crashed into the sea alongside, which they witnessed from the flight deck. However, prior to ditching, the stricken Buccaneer had remained airborne for almost five minutes after the crew had ejected, and during that time it had made two alarming passes at the ship. By 1.30pm the wreckage had been recovered and then Captain Roxburgh learned that

A Scimitar of 800B Flight on the catapult.

(*A. Moore*)

The *Eagle* leaving Singapore with full ceremony as the ship's company man the flight deck. *(Fleet Air Arm Museum)*

top secret mail from the C-in-C Far East Station at Singapore, which had been embarked in the P&O liner *Chitral*, had been diverted to the French colony of Djibouti, on the opposite side of the Gulf of Aden, because of the civil unrest in Aden. Fortunately, a Gannet was able to fly the 150-mile round trip and return to *Eagle* by 6.30pm with its mission successfully completed.

That same afternoon a signal was received from Rear-Admiral Howse requesting that Captain Roxburgh, together with two senior officers, fly ashore for an important conference. Once ashore the three officers were informed that should Mr Ian Smith, the Prime Minister of Rhodesia, declare independence, then the *Eagle* had to be ready to embark a battalion of troops at short notice but, in the meantime, she had to proceed to Mombasa as scheduled for a ten-day self-maintenance period whilst the MoD made a definite decision. On conclusion of the conference Captain Roxburgh and his officers flew back to the *Eagle* and found to their surprise that the carrier was already under way as the main engines had been overheating whilst the ship was at anchor awaiting the return of the CO. That evening the night-flying

programme completed the ship's work-up and FOAC was signalled accordingly thus: 'Work-up completed. We have been fortunate to have achieved in six weeks as much flying as whole of first leg.'

On Tuesday 12 October flying started early and the first launch of the day was a Gannet which was on the forward catapult. However, owing to a technical fault, the aircraft was not boosted but trundled slowly over the forward end of the flight deck with the pilot, Lt Jackson, frantically trying to apply the brakes. To everyone's horror the ship steamed right over the stricken aircraft, but then to the astonishment of all, the three crew members popped up to the surface astern and were safely recovered by the SAR helicopter. During the following afternoon the *Eagle* moored in Kilindini Harbour for the ten-day routine maintenance period. During this time the ship was visited by a Kenyan government minister and on 20 October FOAC, Rear-Admiral H. R. B. Janvrin CB DSC, embarked, together with a large staff, to fly his flag in the carrier.

The *Eagle* left Mombasa during the morning of Saturday 23 October and steamed north, in company with the *Lowestoft*, for the Aden area where she carried out eight

The crew of a Buccaneer prepare for launching.

(A. Moore)

days of flying exercises in conjunction with army units in the colony. On Wednesday 3 November, FOAC struck his flag and then, with his staff, returned to the UK. That evening the *Eagle* left the area and set course for Singapore and the Far East Station. Meanwhile, political events were about to dictate the future movements of the *Eagle* as diplomatic activity in East Africa came to a head.

The dissolution of the Central African Federation in 1963 had left the British Government with the problem of negotiating the independence of Southern Rhodesia, which the whole of the self-governing colony's European population believed to be overdue. However, the majority African populace were hostile to independence being granted to the Rhodesian Front led by Winston Field and no British government was prepared to concede to a party which was opposed to any political concessions to the African majority. In April 1964 Field was replaced as leader of the Rhodesian Front and Prime Minister of Southern Rhodesia by Ian Douglas Smith, a former RAF pilot who had served with distinction in the Battle of Britain, the Western Desert and in Europe. Six months later, when the Labour Government took office in Britain,

any hopes of a reasonable settlement became even more remote and after appointing a sympathetic military commander, Smith called an election at which the European voters overwhelmingly endorsed his intransigence. On 11 November 1965 he issued a unilateral declaration of Rhodesian Independence (UDI) in language which echoed that other famous independence speech of 4 July 1776.

At the time of UDI the *Eagle* was in the Strait of Malacca between Sumatra and Malaya which, in view of the confrontation between Indonesia and Malaysia, was a potentially hostile area. That day most of the serviceable aircraft were flown to RAF Changi, and during the morning of Friday 12 November the *Eagle* made a ceremonial entry into Singapore Naval Base where she secured to B buoy in the Johore Strait. Captain Roxburgh had been assured that UDI would not affect the ship's forthcoming visit to Hong Kong and a number of officers' and ship's company wives had arrived in Singapore, courtesy of RAF Transport Command. It seemed that a routine commission in the Far East lay ahead and that the problems of East Africa were receding.

However, at just after 8am on Thursday 18 November, after only six days in Singapore, Captain Roxburgh received orders to prepare *Eagle* for sea as soon as possible, when she was to proceed to the area of Addu Atoll and the RAF base of Gan in the middle of the Indian Ocean as the political events in East Africa, following UDI, began to affect the movements of troops and naval units. After two very busy days of preparation the *Eagle*, in company with HMS *Brighton*, sailed from Singapore early on the morning of Saturday 20 November and four hours later the embarkation of the aircraft got under way. The third aircraft to land, a Buccaneer, did a 'bolter' and landed in the sea, but fortunately the pilot and observer ejected at only 20ft. Happily both were safely picked up by the SAR helicopter, although the observer suffered back injuries.

After four days steaming through the Indian Ocean the *Eagle* arrived off the island of Gan in the early hours of Wednesday 24 November, and the helicopters were flown ashore to collect the mail. To Captain Roxburgh's surprise they returned with not only mail bags but also Rear-Admiral Janvrin, FOAC, who had left the ship earlier in the month. The necessary signal announcing his arrival was received after FOAC had embarked. Captain Roxburgh was informed that they were to prepare to fly a squadron of Sea Vixens to Ndola in northern Zambia and to set up a defence base in order to forestall any attempts by any other African countries to occupy key areas of Zambia with ostensible offers of 'help' to President Kaunda. The British Prime Minister, Harold Wilson, had rejected the idea of direct military involvement in favour of a policy of calculated ambiguity on the subject, backed by precautionary military movements into Zambia. Next day,

HMS *Eagle* at speed in the Indian Ocean during November 1965. *(Fleet Air Arm Museum)*

as the *Eagle* steamed towards 'Position X', as the launch area was known, preparations for the operation were feverishly under way. In the meantime, however, the question of future defence policy and the RAF island bases versus fleet carriers was highlighted. By 28 November the *Eagle* was stationed 40 miles off Lindi, Tanzania, ready to launch her squadron of 12 Sea Vixen fighter aircraft, together with two Gannet AEW and three Scimitar flight refuelling aircraft, whilst diplomatic activity went on to obtain overflying clearance for ten Javelin aircraft of the RAF's 29 Squadron to fly from Cyprus to Ndola, which was by no means a foregone conclusion. The efficiency and flexibility of the *Eagle* had proved without a doubt the Navy's case in favour of the fixed-wing capability of the Fleet Air Arm. Unfortunately the Press highlighted the RAF role and the *Eagle* received only brief coverage, such as this report in *The Times* newspaper on 2 December 1965: 'A surprise element in the movement of troops to Zambia has been the sudden appearance of the aircraft carrier *Eagle* cruising off Tanzania with several escorts. This emphasizes the advantages and flexibility held by a carrier in the Indian Ocean. The Prime Minister said that HMS *Eagle's* Sea Vixens would have been able to give cover, if necessary,

before the Javelins and their radar arrived. The Sea Vixens would have been hard pressed by distance to have been operational in Zambia, but by being present they might have been able to prevent any other country sending aircraft.' These remarks by the Prime Minister, who ignored the *Eagle's* AEW Gannets and the in-flight refuelling capability of the Scimitars, illustrated which way the senior politicians were thinking about the future of the Fleet Air Arm.

On Friday 3 December, with the arrival of the RAF Javelins and a battalion of British troops in Ndola, the *Eagle* was finally ordered to stand down from the Zambia operation. Captain Roxburgh noted, '...a quiet satisfaction on board that the flexibility of naval air power had been clearly demonstrated and disappointment we had not been allowed to complete the job a full five days earlier.'

From the coast of Tanzania the *Eagle* steamed north to Aden once again, and for 12 days she carried out flying exercises in the area in company with HMS *Dido* and HMS *Salisbury*. On 14 December FOAC hauled down his flag and once again left for the UK. Five days later *Eagle* left the Gulf of Aden bound for Mombasa where she would undergo a three-week self-maintenance period and celebrate Christmas and the New Year.

During the four-day passage to Mombasa the hangar was in great demand by both the ship's aviators, who wanted to carry out non-diversion flying, and by the ship's concert party, who were keen to rehearse for the eagerly awaited concert planned for 22 December. In the event Captain Roxburgh compromised and decreed that all flying would cease on 20 December. Also at this time some unscheduled passengers were embarked from RFA *Tidesurge* - three male stowaways who had been discovered on board just after leaving the Seychelles. They were transferred by jackstay to the *Eagle* where they were held in custody until they could be handed over to the civil authorities in Mombasa. That same evening the ship's concert was held and thoroughly enjoyed by some 2,000 officers and members of the ship's company, who were well entertained until 1am the following morning.

During the afternoon of Thursday 23 December the *Eagle* moored in Kilindini Harbour for her second Christmas at the port, and at the same time, thanks to the efforts of Captain Roxburgh's wife, a number of *Eagle* wives arrived at Nairobi Airport from Singapore, where they had been stranded since late November when the carrier made her sudden departure for the coast of Tanzania. During their stay in Mombasa, Captain and Mrs Roxburgh were invited to a reception in the city at which they met the Kenyan President, Mr Jomo Kenyatta, and Mrs Kenyatta paid a visit to the ship.

On Monday 10 January 1966 the *Eagle* left Mombasa and steamed north once again for Aden and the exercise area off the colony where she undertook flying operations in company with the frigates *Berwick* and *Dido*, and RFA *Tideflow*. This time there was an ITV film crew on board, and for six weeks they had the run of the carrier whilst filming the ship at work. During the exercises over the next few days *Eagle* received visits from Flag Officer Middle East, Rear-Admiral P. N. Howes, the Air Officer Commanding Middle East, Air Vice-Marshal Humphreys, the Flag Officer Naval Air Command, Rear-Admiral D. C. E. F. Gibson, and C-in-C Middle East, Admiral Sir Michael Le Fanu, who was, of course, one of the *Eagle's* former commanding officers. On Saturday 22 January the *Eagle* entered Aden Harbour where a berth had been specially dredged for her, and during their four-day stay the ship's company were able to go ashore and confirm that the place had not improved and that it was still as dry and desolate as it had always been. Even the duty-free shopping at Steamer Point was not easy, with strict security measures in place. There was, therefore, some relief when the carrier left Aden for more exercises off the colony and on Thursday 3 February 100 members of the ship's company left the *Eagle* in Aden Bay for Khormaksar and the UK, while a further 100 joined the ship to take their places. Following this transfer the *Eagle* left Aden for Singapore, in company with the frigates *Chichester* and *Dido*, and the RFAs *Reliant*, *Tidereach*, and *Tidesurge*.

The *Eagle* arrived in Singapore Dockyard on Saturday 12 February 1966 to undertake a 16-day self-maintenance period. Two days later, on the BBC World Service radio news, it was announced that the Navy's fixed-wing carriers were to be scrapped and that the Admiralty Board had resigned. However, although this proved to be a somewhat inaccurate rumour, the following week the new FOAC, Rear-Admiral W. D. O' Brien, arrived in Singapore to fly his flag in the *Eagle* and he was able to give details of the long-awaited Defence Review including the announcement that the Navy's fixed-wing aircraft carriers were to be phased out within ten years. Next day the news was made public and that morning Captain Roxburgh addressed the ship's company on the matter of the immediate cancellation of the proposed new 54,000-ton fleet carrier CVA-01, and the proposal to scrap the remaining four aircraft carriers, *Eagle*, *Ark Royal*, *Victorious* and *Hermes*, by early 1976. This naturally caused a great deal of consternation and anxiety amongst a large proportion of the *Eagle's* officers and ship's company, even though Captain Roxburgh stressed that there was unlikely to be a sudden rundown of aircrew and maintenance staff as a result of what he described as, and what subsequently proved to be, a disastrous policy.

During the ship's stay at Singapore the ITV film crew left for the UK and the subsequent production, entitled 'Warship Eagle', was shown on national television that summer. The *Eagle* herself left Singapore on Monday 28 February for six days of flying exercises off the west coast of Malaya and the island of Penang. On 5 March orders were received to steam across the Indian Ocean to Gan in preparation for relieving the *Ark Royal* which had already started to enforce the United Nations oil sanctions against Rhodesia by patrolling the waters of the Mozambique Channel to prevent unauthorized tankers from entering the port of Beira, which was Rhodesia's main outlet in what was then a Portuguese colony.

During 9/10 March the squadrons underwent refresher flying practice off Gan, which was necessary after the 16-day SMP in Singapore. Over the two days 110 sorties were flown and, in addition, the *Eagle's* first three-ship RAS took place with the RFAs *Reliant* and *Tidepool*. During the operation 1,440 tons of fuel oil and 131 tons of stores were transferred in two and a half hours. The *Eagle* arrived on the Middle East Station on 11 March and four days later, on the morning of 15 March, she rendezvoused with the *Ark Royal* to take over the Beira Patrol. Soon afterwards the two carriers were manoeuvred in close company in order that photographs could be taken, before the *Ark Royal* steamed north and left the area. At 7pm that evening the first aircraft, an AEW Gannet, was launched to commence the *Eagle's* surveillance operations in the area. It was of some satisfaction to all those in the *Eagle* to learn that originally RAF Shackleton aircraft, to be based on Mombasa, were to have carried out the air surveillance tasks, but they had not been able to meet the commitment and, once again, the Fleet Air Arm had come to the rescue.

The units under Captain Roxburgh's command at that time consisted of the destroyer *Cambrian* and the frigate *Plymouth*, which patrolled close inshore off Beira and reported all ships entering and leaving the port, and the RFAs *Reliant*, *Resurgent* and *Tidepool* which provided a shuttle service between Mombasa and the operational area. It was the *Eagle's* duty to survey an area up to a distance of 250 miles from a position 100 miles east of Beira, in order to identify and report all oil tankers which were approaching the port. The RAF Shackletons based in Mombasa were of little value for surveillance duties, but they were useful when it came to mail deliveries.

During the morning of 17 March one of the *Eagle's* aircraft detected the first suspected blockade runner, the Naess-Holm Line tanker, MV *Enterprise*. She had left the Persian Gulf fully laden with oil and her course showed that she was heading directly for Beira. However, when intercepted by *Eagle* later that day, she stated that she was bound for the River Plate and so she was sent on her way with a friendly 'bon voyage!'

By 20 March the RAF Shackletons had been relocated to a base at Majunga (Mahajanga) in Madagascar, but it was still clear that they were unable to enforce the oil blockade and it became apparent that the *Eagle's* stint on the Beira Patrol was going to be a long one. On 22 March Captain Roxburgh was informed that the carrier would not be returning to Singapore until 10 May, which was 71 days after she had left the Naval Base. He immediately passed this news to the ship's company who took it quite cheerfully as, by this time, everyone had settled down to the routine of the patrol. The main complaint was the lack of publicity which all their hard work was receiving and the misrepresentation of their role by the UK Press, whilst the RAF got much more than their fair share of credit. This included reports and photographs of 'RAF' Gannets overflying ships in the Mozambique Channel, complete with Royal Navy and *Eagle* markings clearly visible. Without doubt this reflected the political priorities which prevailed at the highest level in the Government at that time. It therefore came as no surprise to Captain Roxburgh when, during the patrol, he saw a letter in *The Times* from one of the young aircrew officers neatly voicing the feelings of all. The Captain had, perforce, to express his displeasure to the officer concerned for breaking the rules in writing to the Press on sensitive matters without permission. Nevertheless, there was no doubting that the officer was held in great esteem by his brother officers.

At the end of March reports were being received of a suspected blockade runner, the MV *Joanna V*, and it was

not long before the *Eagle's* aircraft had located the vessel. Captain Roxburgh ordered the frigate HMS *Plymouth* to intercept her, which she did. However, there was no United Nations sanction of the use of force by the Navy in order to secure compliance, and the ship's master was a very determined man who was, by coincidence, a retired Royal Hellenic naval commander and a former member of the NATO staff in Malta where he had served with Captain Fanshawe of HMS *Plymouth*. The *Joanna V* did eventually anchor off Beira and inside territorial waters, despite determined personal efforts by Captain Fanshawe who boarded the vessel in an attempt to prevent it from doing so.

Next day a report was received on board *Eagle* that another suspected blockade runner, the MV *Manuella*, was making her way to Beira with a cargo of oil, and one of her Sea Vixens soon sighted the vessel in the Mozambique Channel in a position Lat 15° - 15'S/Long 41° - 15'E and making for Beira at 13 knots. Captain Roxburgh ordered the *Berwick*, which had relieved the *Plymouth*, to intercept the tanker. When asked for her destination she signalled to the frigate that she had left the Persian Gulf and was bound for Durban and Rotterdam. During the time that the warships were engaged in the interception of the suspect vessel, the *Eagle* received an SOS from another tanker, the *Esso Spain*, requesting medical assistance. The *Eagle* rendezvoused with the vessel at 1pm on 7 April and transferred a doctor, who was able to successfully treat a member of the crew suffering from a kidney complaint.

During 8 April the *Berwick* accompanied the *Manuella* on her southerly course towards Durban, and she finally left her at the southern end of the Mozambique Channel as she headed towards the South African port. However, although the frigate had returned to the patrol area off Beira, the *Eagle's* aircraft kept the tanker under observation and soon afterwards a Sea Vixen reported that the *Manuella* had reversed her course and was heading once again for Beira. As the *Berwick* was refuelling, the frigate HMS *Puma* was ordered to close the rogue tanker for a second time and on this occasion, following the United Nations approval of the use of force to stop tankers entering Beira, there would be no repeat of the *Joanna V's* blatant refusal to cooperate. Whilst the *Puma* was standing by the *Manuella*, a liner passed the two ships and in answer to its signal, 'What ship?' the tanker replied, '*Manuella* escorted by *Puma*', to which the liner retorted, 'Be good!' Shortly afterwards the Greek tanker received orders from her owners to proceed to Durban, and after being shadowed by *Puma* and tracked by the *Eagle's* aircraft, the *Manuella* arrived at the port on the morning of 12 April. However, as before, the Press coverage of the two incidents played down the Fleet Air Arm's hard work while highlighting the RAF Shackleton's more marginal effort.

During the *Eagle's* patrol there were many light-hearted moments and one such occasion involved an exchange of

The *Eagle* refuelling from RFA *Tidepool* (port side), and transferring stores from RFA *Reliant* in April 1966, whilst enforcing the oil blockade of Beira.

(Fleet Air Arm Museum)

signals with the Glen Line merchant ship *Stirlingshire*, which had obviously been of much interest to *Eagle's* aircraft, as the following was received by the carrier:

'*The holocausts of noise and fire*
have thrice disturbed our hours of sleep.
So please desist while we retire
and on the deck your planes please keep.'

Not to be outdone, *Eagle's* budding poets were quickly off the mark with their reply which was swiftly sent back to the *Stirlingshire*:

'*Apologies for noise and fire*
which obviously has raised your ire.
But oil embargo we must keep
regardless of the need to sleep.'

On 17 April, just as the *Eagle's* ship's company were looking forward to the *Ark Royal* taking over the patrol once again, a signal was received stating that the latter had been delayed in Singapore with mechanical problems and that the *Eagle* would be required to remain on station for at least two weeks longer than had been scheduled. In the event she was released from the Beira Patrol on 30 April, without having to wait for the *Ark Royal*, and the last flights of the patrol were undertaken that morning. It was ironic that the *Eagle's* final task of the patrol was to carry out a request which had been received from MoD (Air), via MoD (Navy) to provide a mosaic and large-scale oblique photographic reconnaissance cover of Aldabra, which was one of the RAF's cherished projects for a future island base once the Navy's carriers were no more. The ship was fortunate to be able to mount four very successful Buccaneer sorties on the morning of 2 May when she passed 100 miles to the south-east of Aldabra, as the area clouded over shortly after the aircraft arrived. The comprehensive results were signalled to MoD (Navy) the same day and Captain Roxburgh could not resist a final sentence: 'Greater love hath no carrier than this.' The higher reaches of the MoD (Navy) thought this comment rather flippant, but it was much appreciated by the RAF.

After handing over command of the patrol to Captain S. L. McArdle RN, in HMS *Mohawk*, the *Eagle* set course for Singapore and a long-awaited SMP in the Naval Dockyard. On the afternoon of Wednesday 4 May she rendezvoused with the *Ark Royal* and transferred three Scimitars and a Gannet, in order to make up her aircraft complement, and on 9 May nine aircraft were launched to RAF Changi. Next day, as the carrier arrived off the island, the C-in-C Far East Station, Admiral Sir Frank Twiss KCB, embarked by helicopter to welcome her back. Soon after this the *Eagle* secured alongside in the Naval Base for a 21-day self-maintenance period.

During her stint on the Beira Patrol the *Eagle* had been at sea for 71 days and she had steamed 30,000 miles, including her passage to and from Singapore. Her aircrews had flown 1,880 sorties and they had covered a daily area of 200,000 square miles during their surveillance operations. They had identified 767 ships, including 116 oil tankers, and the *Eagle* herself had monitored 1,200 radio messages from merchant vessels. It had been a magnificent effort and in his official report Captain Roxburgh stated: 'In conclusion I must place on record my pride and gratitude in being the Commanding Officer of such men, such machines and such a ship at such a time.'

Following her maintenance period the *Eagle* left Singapore on the morning of Wednesday 1 June for three days of exercises, before setting course for Hong Kong. She secured to No 1 buoy in Victoria Harbour on 7 June and four days later, as she was about to sail for the Beira Patrol again, a signal was received stating that aircraft carriers were no longer required for these duties. For the ship's company this brought the unexpected bonus of two extra days in the colony whilst the programme was reorganized. However, this coincided with torrential rainstorms in the area and when the *Eagle* sailed for the US Navy's Subic Bay exercise areas on Monday 13 June, six of her helicopters remained behind for a few hours to assist with the flood relief work. The *Eagle* spent 11 days exercising in the South China Sea with the US Navy, who had pulled out all the stops to help, including flying three F8 Crusader aircraft from Japan to act as target-towing and target aircraft. On 15 June a Sea Vixen, flown by Sub-Lt Parrett RN, made a successful emergency landing into the crash barrier with only one wheel, without serious damage to the aircraft. This was preferable to diverting the aircraft to the US naval airfield ashore with all the attendant back-up problems which might arise after the *Eagle* had left the area. Nine days later, on Friday 24 June, a Gannet was lost when its engine failed, but happily the crew were recovered safely.

During the first two weeks of July the *Eagle* underwent a further maintenance period at Singapore and it was during this time that the tenth and last aircraft of the deployment was lost. Sadly both the pilot, Sub-Lt Parrett RN, of the successful one wheel landing into the crash barrier off Subic, and the observer, Lt Woodford RN, were killed when their Sea Vixen crashed during night-flying exercises from RAF Changi.

The *Eagle* left Singapore for the last time during the commission on Tuesday 12 July for exercises off Penang, and two days later the Rt Hon Denis Healey, the Secretary of State for Defence, visited the ship. During his visit to the carrier he addressed the officers in the wardroom and, given the Government's decision to run down the Fleet Air Arm, it was understandable that his reception was polite, but decidedly cool. When he injudiciously referred to the RAF having moved in quickly to Ndola he was swiftly and firmly corrected.

On the morning of Sunday 17 July a memorial service was held on the quarterdeck, in between flying operations, for Lt Woodford and Sub-Lt Parrett who had both been cremated ashore; on conclusion of the service their ashes were scattered over the sea. Two days later, with the programme of exercises completed, the *Eagle* left the Malacca Strait and set course for Mombasa where everyone could enjoy five days of rest and relaxation.

It was on Tuesday 26 July that the *Eagle* moored in Kilindini Harbour and she remained there until the last day of the month when she left the port bound for Suez and home. On Monday 1 August the *Eagle* crossed the equator for the eighth time during the second leg of the commission and, at last, there was time to hold the 'Crossing the Line' ceremony. Next day came, what was, for many, one of the highlights of the deployment when the *Eagle* rendezvoused with the *Victorious*, which was outbound from Portsmouth to relieve the *Eagle* as the 'East of Suez' aircraft carrier. On Saturday 6 August the *Eagle* made her northbound transit of the Suez Canal and three days later she put into Malta's Grand Harbour for a four-day visit. On Sunday 14 August, en route from Malta to Gibraltar, 12 Sea Vixens, eight Buccaneers and four Scimitars were launched to their UK stations and all of them were home within two hours. After spending four days in Gibraltar, where there were further opportunities for rest and relaxation, the *Eagle* secured alongside at Devonport Dockyard at 10am on Monday 22 August 1966. During the 12 months which she had spent in foreign waters, most of them east of Suez, she had been at sea for 248 days and she had steamed 108,000 miles.

During this period her aircraft had operated in support of the local forces in Aden which were carrying out internal security duties. She had operated off the coast of East Africa following UDI by the Government of Rhodesia, and her aircraft had been poised to fly into Zambia prior to the later arrival of RAF aircraft. From March until May 1966 she had operated the oil blockade of Rhodesia, spending 71 continuous days at sea, which was a post-war record for one of HM Ships. Her aircraft had located the two blockade runners *Joanna V* and *Manuella* and she had coordinated the interception of the two tankers. Finally, in Hong Kong, her helicopters had assisted the civil powers during the disastrous floods in the colony in June 1966.

Without doubt she had positively projected the Navy's flexibility and, despite the politicians, she had demonstrated that she was a force to be reckoned with.

On her arrival back in the UK there were almost 3,000 relatives and friends waiting to greet her and there was leave to look forward to. It was also the end of the commission and for most members of the ship's company this meant that draft chits would soon be received.

The *Eagle* herself went into extended notice for steam as the dockyard took her over for a seven-month refit, and the remaining members of the ship's company moved to the carrier HMS *Centaur*, which was in use as an accommodation ship. It was the end of a very successful commission.

A dramatic view of a Sea Vixen as it approaches the *Eagle's* flight deck. *(Fleet Air Arm Museum)*

HMS *Eagle* undergoing full-power trials.   *(W. J. Pilgrim)*

On completion of repairs following her boiler room fire, the *Eagle* was able to put to sea again and on Sunday 28 May 1967, when she was 20 miles from Plymouth, the carrier rendezvoused with Francis Chichester as he neared the end of his epic single-handed voyage round the world in his yacht *Gypsy Moth IV*. Apart from watchkeepers, the entire ship's company gathered on the flight deck to cheer, and the yachtsman responded by dipping his White Ensign to the carrier.

(Captain H. Owen)

Chapter Eleven

Fifth Commission - Withdrawal From Aden

During the summer of 1966, as the *Eagle* lay alongside Devonport Dockyard, she was opened to the public during Navy Days and she proved to be the star attraction, with long queues of visitors waiting patiently to look over her.

During her refit the *Eagle* had been equipped with a single DAX II arrester wire in preparation for trials of the McDonnell Douglas Phantom FGI general-purpose fighter which had been ordered for service with both the *Eagle* and the *Ark Royal*. However, it was the fitting for trial of only one such arrester wire which was to cause the *Eagle's* early demise for, upon the ship's return to operational service, the *Ark Royal* was taken in hand for a three and a half-year refit during which she too was modernized, and although it was to only 85% of the *Eagle's* standard, she was fitted with a complete set of DAX II arrester wires and it was this factor which enabled the *Ark Royal* to continue in operational service until the late 1970s.

The *Eagle* at speed during her operational work-up.
(Captain H. Owen)

On Monday 28 November 1966 the *Eagle* recommissioned with a new ship's company, with the final draft party arriving eight days later. On 8 December Captain Roxburgh addressed the ship's company in *Centaur's* hangar, but it was not until Wednesday 14 March 1967 that everyone moved back to the *Eagle* which, after the accommodation ship, seemed like comparative luxury. There then followed three weeks of hard work as the ship was prepared for sea.

Commissioning Day was Thursday 6 April 1967 and some 2,800 of the ship's company's families and friends came down to the dockyard for the occasion. Captain Roxburgh read the Commissioning Warrant and after reading the telegram of loyal greetings to Her Majesty The Queen and her reply, he addressed those assembled on the important role which the services, and the Navy in particular, had to play in society as a whole, not only in defence but in maintaining high standards and self discipline. He outlined details of the *Eagle's* sea trials which were to take place over the following weeks and he continued, keeping in mind the Government's decision to phase out fixed-wing aircraft carriers within ten years: 'Whatever may be the future in ten years time or more of such a wonderful ship as this, I would like to assure everyone here that the *Eagle* and her sister aircraft carriers, and the Fleet Air Arm as a whole, have a wholly worthwhile job to perform. Such ships and their aircraft form, in my opinion, probably the single most potent, versatile and flexible instrument of government policy that there is - and let no one forget this.'

Two days after the commissioning ceremony, at 5.45pm on Saturday 8 April, the *Eagle* slipped from her berth and steamed through Plymouth Sound to C buoy where she secured to prepare for the three weeks of sea trials. Three days later, at 9am on Tuesday 11 April, the *Eagle* sailed from the Sound and later that same day, at 4.20pm, when the ship was on the Looe measured mile, a serious electrical fire broke out in B boiler room uptake space which quickly took hold. Emergency fire parties were swiftly on the scene, but despite their best efforts it was not extinguished until 8pm that evening. During the fire-fighting operations Petty Officer Ordnance Electrician John Latham, who was assisting Lt Austin to gain access to the compartment, by rigging ventilation fans and emergency lighting, made a thorough survey of the uptake space and he was able to prevent the fire parties from spraying sea water on electrical cables which had been burned through, thereby saving serious injury and, perhaps, even loss of life among the

A Sea Vixen is launched from the waist catapult, while the Wessex planeguard helicopter hovers nearby. *(W. J. Pilgrim)*

hose teams. At the time the heat in the compartment was so intense that water on the deck was turning instantly to steam, and molten metal was actually dripping from the deckhead. However, in spite of these difficulties and without protective clothing, he continued to lead the firefighters and for his prompt actions he was awarded the BEM. Eventually the fire was extinguished but it was 10pm before the ship's senior engineer officer, Commander A. M. J. Cumming RN, and senior electrical officer, Commander A. A. Murphy RN, were able to enter the compartment to assess the damage, which proved to be serious. Nevertheless, even though the carrier was reduced to two shafts on four boilers, she remained at sea for another two days in order to complete radar trials and to enable the dockyard to prepare for her unexpected return.

Finally, on Thursday 13 April, still on only two shafts and four boilers and attended by the tug *Sea Giant*, with two more tugs standing by, the *Eagle* returned to Devonport for repairs to her damaged machinery compartment.

At noon on Thursday 4 May, during the time she was alongside, there was a change of command as Captain J. E. Pope RN relieved Rear-Admiral Roxburgh, who had been appointed Flag Officer Sea Training. The repairs to the fire-damaged boiler room took six weeks, but with ten days' leave having been granted to each watch there were no complaints. During the enforced stay the children of Nazareth House Children's Home visited the ship and they were presented with a large television set by the ship's company. Nazareth House had, over a number of years, received many gifts and much assistance from the *Eagle's*

A Buccaneer on the catapult.
(W. J. Pilgrim)

'Crossing the Line' ceremony on 30 August 1967, as the *Eagle* steams south to Cape Town.

(Captain H. Owen)

ship's company and they had always shown their appreciation of the friendship by making a point of turning out to wave farewell and to greet the carrier as she negotiated the Hamoaze. Each time the *Eagle* steamed by the children would cheer the ship and wave their sheets from the garden of the Home, a gesture which was much appreciated by all on board the *Eagle*.

It was Saturday 27 May when the boiler room repairs were completed and the *Eagle* was able to put to sea again, and at 5pm the following day she rendezvoused with Francis Chichester as he neared the end of his epic single-handed voyage round the world in his yacht *Gipsy Moth IV*. The meeting took place about 20 miles from Plymouth where *Gipsy Moth IV* was being escorted by the *Brave Borderer* and *Brave Swordsman*, who were keeping at bay a host of private craft. The *Eagle* approached to within 200 yards of the yacht and the entire ship's company, apart from the watchkeepers, gathered on the flight deck to give three rousing cheers as the Navy's biggest warship steamed by the small vessel. The yachtsman responded by going aft to dip his White Ensign to the carrier. Captain Hugh Owen

remembers that, although the *Gipsy Moth's* hull was clearly showing signs of its record voyage, the sails were perfectly white and still immaculate.

As soon as the *Eagle's* trials were completed she returned to Devonport where she spent ten days alongside whilst essential repairs and adjustments were made. In late June, after embarking the ground parties of 800 Buccaneer Squadron, 899 Sea Vixen Squadron, 849D Gannet Flight, together with the personnel and the Wessex helicopters of 820 Squadron, the *Eagle* sailed once again to complete her operational work-up. 800 Squadron had, only three months previously, carried out the bombing of the wrecked Liberian oil tanker *Torrey Canyon*, which had grounded on the Pollards Rock off Land's End and produced a disastrous oil slick covering an area of almost 300 square miles. The squadron's action helped to reduce the environmental damage caused by the oil spill.

Also embarked in the *Eagle* as she left Devonport were the Mayor of Exeter, Alderman R. C. Board, and four of his civic officials, who were on board to witness the day's flying operations. However, when the time came for them

'Procedure Alpha' as the *Eagle* enters Cape Town on 8 September 1967, a windy day with a choppy sea.

(Captain H. Owen)

Middle East where she was to be on hand when the colony of Aden achieved independence, which was scheduled for 29 November 1967.

The ship's departure from the UK was fixed for late August, and in order that she could leave home waters fully stored after her exercises the largest vertical replenishment programme ('vertrep') ever planned was carried out. The operation took place on Friday 25 August, shortly before the *Eagle* sailed for the Far East, by way of Cape Town, and she was due to RAS from the RFA *Resource*. However, the *Resource* had suffered mechanical problems and she was unable to leave Devonport Dockyard under her own power so, in the event, she was towed round to Plymouth Sound where the *Eagle* was at anchor. Once there the storing commenced and over 100 tons were transferred in 169 loads by the helicopters of 820 Squadron, assisted by helicopters from the RFAs *Regent* and *Resource*. Once on board the stores were rapidly passed below decks by the large stores party which had been mustered and by 2pm that day the *Eagle* was fully operational again.

The *Eagle's* long voyage south was certainly no summer cruise as stormy weather seemed to follow the ship as she steamed through the Atlantic Ocean. As she crossed the equator King Neptune and his court made their traditional visit and the ceremonies were held as the carrier 'Crossed the Line'. As she steamed into the South Atlantic for the first time in her career the heavy ocean swells made life somewhat uncomfortable. There was a short halt off Ascension Island during which she met the US Navy's carrier USS *Forrestal*, which was on her way home from the waters off Vietnam where she had suffered a disastrous fire in which nearly 100 men lost their lives. The *Eagle* was to be the first British aircraft carrier to call at Cape Town for six years and, of course, with the Suez Canal closed after the Arab-Israeli Six-Day War, it emphasized the strategic importance of the Cape route to the Far East.

After ploughing through particularly heavy seas as she approached the port, the *Eagle* arrived in Table Bay at 8am on Friday 8 September and, after firing a 21-gun national salute, she was assisted to her berth at the port's Duncan Dock. Captain Pope then left to call on the C-in-C of the South African Navy, Vice-Admiral H. H. Biermann, as the first of his official visits. The *Eagle's* stay at Cape Town coincided with a particularly cold winter at the Cape and there was even snow on Table Mountain. A nostalgic reminder of home came with a special request from the Mayor for the *Eagle's* cooks to bake some genuine 'tiddy oggies', which of course they were able to do. The visit to the South African port was a great success, with over 10,000 people going to look round the carrier, and when she sailed well over 1,000 residents came to wave goodbye. Unfortunately, the main publicity in the Press concerned six members of the ship's company who had decided not to return to the ship. Two of them were subsequently found

to return to Exeter in one of the ship's helicopters, thick fog was covering the ship's operating area which meant they were stranded on board. The *Eagle* herself, working to a tight schedule, was unable to wait for the weather to clear and she had to leave for the Moray Firth to carry out further exercises off the coast of Scotland. Fortunately, the initial concern which the guests felt soon turned to enjoyment and when they finally left the ship on 26 June, after three days on board, they felt quite at home in the carrier.

After embarking the fixed-wing aircraft off Lossiemouth there followed three weeks of hard work, which culminated in the ship's Operational Readiness Inspection off Brawdy by FOAC, Rear-Admiral L. D. Empson, who had, in fact, been the *Eagle's* first commanding officer following her modernization in 1964. Having passed her inspection everyone on board was looking forward to joint exercises in the Atlantic with the US Navy, followed by a visit to Boston, Massachusetts. However, this was not to be for it had been decided that the ship was, instead, to head for the

Eagle approaching her berth in Cape Town harbour.

(*W. J. Pilgrim*)

The *Eagle* is about to embark stores from RFA *Reliant*.

(*Captain H. Owen*)

The naval task force off Aden in November 1967. *Eagle* leads HM Ships *London, Ajax, Albion* and *Minerva*.

(*W. J. Pilgrim*)

to have stowed away in a nurses' home.

Once at sea the *Eagle* carried out exercises with the South African Navy, although a large part of the flying programme had to be cancelled because of the heavy ocean swells. Following this she set courses for the long haul across the Indian Ocean to Singapore, breaking the voyage for flying exercises off Gan, a rather desolate island which forms part of Addu Atoll, the most southerly group of the Maldive Islands. At that time the RAF had a base and an airstrip on the island and during the flying operations one of the carrier's Sea Vixens, which had been diverted to the RAF base, overshot the runway on landing and ended up in the shallow waters of the lagoon, 20 feet from the shoreline. Fortunately, both crew members were uninjured and the aircraft was recovered and returned to the ship by lighter after the *Eagle* had anchored in Addu Atoll lagoon.

Whilst the *Eagle* was off Gan, FO2 FES, Rear-Admiral E. B. Ashmore, hoisted his flag in the carrier and after several days of flying operations, the *Eagle* set course for Singapore. The serviceable aircraft were flown off to RAF

Changi and RNAS Simbang and the *Eagle* arrived in the Singapore Naval Base on Friday 6 October for a 17-day self-maintenance period and, of course, the pleasures of Singapore's swimming pools and 'Tiger' beer. It was also an opportunity to send parcels home in time for Christmas.

The *Eagle* left Singapore on Monday 23 October, for a nine-week patrol off the barren rocks of Aden as part of the task force which was covering the withdrawal of British forces prior to the colony becoming independent. By that time the internal security measures consisted of protection of the base areas as the rival nationalist organizations, the NLF and FLOSY, conducted a vicious campaign against each other as they fought to gain power in South Arabia. It had become apparent that the NLF was in a dominant position, but it was also clear that there was very little prospect of a stable government being in power when the British left. In early November, as the *Eagle* arrived off the coast of Aden, the Foreign Secretary, Mr Michael Stewart, announced that the date of the final British withdrawal had been brought forward from 'early 1968' to late November

HM Ships *Eagle, Albion, London, Ajax* and *Minerva* off Aden. *(Fleet Air Arm Museum)*

1967, thus prompting the two rival factions in the colony to resume their violent struggle with even more brutality. The decisive factor in this internal struggle was the decision of the South Arabian Army (SAA) to back the NLF, which provided some sort of stability as the final plans for the British departure were put into place. The RAF's commitment to assist the SAA on the border with Yemen continued throughout October, with sorties being flown by Hawker Hunters from RAF Khormaksar. However, as the last RAF aircraft left the base, this air defence role was taken over on 7 November by the Buccaneers and Sea Vixens from the *Eagle*, with HMS *Albion's* helicopters providing the final link with Khormaksar. As the *Eagle's* aircraft assumed the protective task from the RAF, the carrier's radar provided the early warning cover for both the forces ashore and for the naval task force which had assembled. From the morning of Sunday 26 November, whilst the mammoth job of pulling out the majority of the remaining troops was carried out, 899 Squadron kept four Sea Vixens airborne and constantly circling RAF Khormaksar in case air support was needed. Despite the fact that Aden had always been regarded by the RAF as 'their territory', 899's Sea Vixens had the honour of being

the last British fighter aircraft to fly over that desolate tip of South Arabia. Once again the Fleet Air Arm's power and flexibility had been visibly demonstrated but, as before, the politicians chose to ignore it.

The only independence 'ceremonial' which took place in Aden was on 28 November, the day of the final withdrawal, when the Governor, Sir Humphrey Trevelyan, who had vacated Government House the day before and had spent the night on board the *Eagle*, flew ashore and with the C-in-C, Admiral Sir Michael Le Fanu, inspected a Joint Services Guard of Honour at RAF Khormaksar. Then, as Sir Humphrey boarded the RAF transport aircraft which was to take him back to the UK, the *Eagle's* Royal Marines Band struck up 'Fings Ain't Wot They Used To Be'. It was not traditional music for an independence ceremony, but it was very appropriate for that occasion.

The final departure from Aden took place at just before 3pm that day when 42 Commando's rearguard units were withdrawn by helicopter from their defensive positions and flown to HMS *Albion*. The very last man to leave was Lt-Col Morgan who was flown to the *Eagle* where he handed over command to Rear-Admiral Ashmore. The British in Aden had been successors to the Ottoman Empire, and 28

Eagle transfers stores from RFA *Stromness. (Captain H. Owen)*

November 1967 saw the end of 128 years of British rule. The final withdrawal ranks as one of the best planned and executed operations in military history and the *Eagle*, her ship's company and squadrons played no small part in what was a difficult task. During the weeks that the *Eagle* had spent in the waters of the Gulf of Aden the ship's company had amused themselves, between flying operations, with deck sports, a boxing tournament, a handicrafts exhibition and a 'Sods Opera' and, to make everything bearable, the Gannets of 849D Flight had provided a regular postal service as well as keeping watch on all shipping in the area.

Following the final withdrawal, the naval task force remained in Aden's territorial waters for nine hours until midnight on 28/29 November when South Arabia officially became independent, after which the *Eagle* set course for Singapore where she arrived on Saturday 2 December 1967, in good time for the Christmas celebrations. The highlight of the ship's menu over the festive season was the Christmas pudding which had been made from half a ton of ingredients including one gallon of rum - not even the tropical heat of Singapore diminished the appetites for that delicacy or for the ever popular 'chips' which the various galleys produced by the ton and without newspaper wrappings.

During her stay in Singapore many of *Eagle's* ship's

company took the opportunity of station leave and travelled to Penang, the Cameron Highlands and Frasers Hill. There was even a proposed expedition to Kota Tinggi in Central Johore, but unfortunately this venture was washed out by the torrential rains of the seasonal north-west monsoon which caused widespread flooding in south Malaya. At the beginning of January 1968 there came the depressing announcement that the Royal Navy's carrier force was likely to be disbanded completely in early 1970, and that it was unlikely that the *Eagle* would have any further modifications to equip her completely for Phantom aircraft. Although the Navy's order for 40 Phantoms could not be cancelled, it was announced that they, together with the Buccaneers, would be handed over to the RAF.

After four weeks of well-earned rest the *Eagle* left Singapore and re-embarked her aircraft in the Malacca Strait before carrying out a short period of flying practice off Penang. Following this the carrier set course west across the Indian Ocean, once again to the area off Gan where she took part in 'Exercise Partner' which involved 21 ships, including Australian and New Zealand Navy frigates and the brand new nuclear attack submarine HMS *Warspite*. At the end of the exercise the *Eagle* steamed south-east for over 2,000 miles arriving at Fremantle in Western Australia

The naval task force off Aden prepares for a final steam-past. *Left to Right - Back Row:* RFAs *Retainer, Tidespring* and *Reliant. Centre Row: Eagle, Albion, Intrepid* and *Anchorite. Front Row: London* and *Ajax.*
(*Captain H. Owen*)

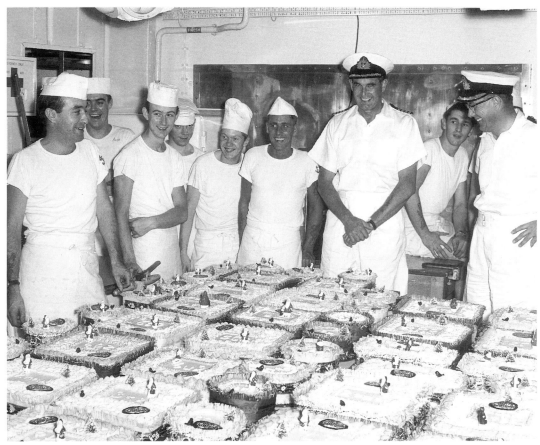

Christmas in Singapore and the ship's bakery has produced a cake for each mess deck. *(Captain H. Owen)*

on Monday 12 February for a 15-day visit. On the previous day, when the ship was 200 miles from the port, six Buccaneers, six Sea Vixens and three Gannets were flown off to the RAAF base at Pearce, 50 miles from Fremantle, in order that they could continue flying practice whilst the ship was berthed alongside. Before landing they flew in formation over Perth and Fremantle which was appreciated by the residents of both cities. On her first evening in the Australian port a reception was held for 800 local people in the hangar and on St Valentine's Day there was a ship's dance at Fremantle's Pagoda Ballroom. It was well attended by 1,500 members of the ship's company, who were greatly outnumbered by 2,000 Australian girls, and with two bands and a good supply of 'Swan' lager, the evening was a great success. Other events which made *Eagle* a very popular visitor to the city were a children's party for 400 young guests with a funfair on the flight deck, and a performance of the ship's concert, 'Alan Laddin', for disabled ex-servicemen in Perth.

The visit to Fremantle ended at 9 am on Tuesday 27 February when *Eagle* left harbour to embark her squadrons and set course for the Cocos Islands, where her aircraft

practised landings on the RAAF air base. The *Eagle*, together with RFA *Olwen*, left the area on Wednesday 6 April and set course for the Sunda Strait between the islands of Java and Sumatra. At 4.30pm on Saturday 9 April, off the coast of Java, Lt John Heath fell overboard from the flight deck whilst playing a game of deck hockey. Fortunately, the rescue helicopter was soon on the scene and he was picked up safely after having been in the water for about eight minutes. The opposing team denied hotly that they had been trying to eliminate the opposition to gain an advantage!

Soon after her arrival in the South China Sea the *Eagle* headed for the island of Pulau Tioman off the east coast of Malaya, which is now, in fact, an exclusive holiday destination. Here the usual banyan leave was taken, with the beaches providing sufficient enjoyment for most of those who ventured ashore. A few adventurous souls, however, decided to forgo the easy life and set off instead on expeditions into the hilly jungle areas at the centre of the island. For those who did not wish to leave the 'comfort' of the ship there was a full-scale race meeting on the flight deck, complete with totalisator and bookies.

Following the weekend of relaxation the *Eagle* began ten days of intensive flying exercises which were interspersed with gunnery and anti-submarine exercises. On completion of these the ship sailed across the South China Sea to Hong Kong, where she arrived with full ceremony on Friday 22 March. Although the weather was somewhat dull and damp, the opportunity for rest and recreation was welcomed by everyone and the Padre organized a number of visits into the New Territories and to the Chinese border.

After leaving Hong Kong on Saturday 6 April, *Eagle* arrived two days later in the US Navy's exercise areas off their naval base at Subic bay, where many were looking forward to spending Easter enjoying the dubious pleasures of Olongapo, but it was not to be. No sooner had the exercises started than a signal was received ordering the *Eagle* to proceed towards the Arabian Sea. Once again the politics of the Middle East had altered the course of the commission. Following Aden's independence from Britain, negotiations had been going on between the government of

the former colony and Whitehall regarding monetary compensation which the South Arabian Government thought was due to them from the former colonial power. However, the difference between what they thought they should get and what the British Government actually offered to them was so great that it was clear there was going to be no quick settlement. The negotiations were acrimonious and it was thought that they would break down without any solution having been reached, giving rise to concern about the safety of the British employees who still worked in the BP oil refinery at Little Aden, which had continued to operate following the withdrawal. Therefore it had been decided at government level to form a naval task force which could, at short notice, take action to forestall any hostile moves towards the British nationals, or rescue them from their isolated position in the former British colony. The force was formed in great secrecy and they were ordered to stand by in a very remote area of the Indian Ocean, well away from the normal shipping lanes where

During *Eagle's* visit to Fremantle in February 1968 long queues of visitors waited patiently to tour the ship.   *(W. J. Pilgrim)*

The *Eagle* arrives at Hong Kong on 22 March 1968.   *(W. J. Pilgrim)*

their presence might be noted and reported by passing Soviet ships. Rear-Admiral Ashmore christened his force 'Point Patience' which, as the weeks dragged by, was considered very appropriate. Once again the ship returned to a seemingly endless routine of plying the same route around a hot and featureless area of the Arabian Sea and, between flying exercises, the flight deck was given over to race meetings, and an 'Eagle Tattoo', with its own version of the renowned field gun display and, of courses, the 'buzzes' ran round the ship one after the other, with Singapore and Mombasa being top of the list for future destinations.

Fortunately, neither of these were correct and after handing over to the *Albion*, the *Eagle* left the area to return home to Devonport, again by way of Cape Town. On Saturday 1 June, eight weeks after leaving Hong Kong, the *Eagle* steamed back into Table Bay and alongside her berth in Duncan Dock. Once again the hospitality was lavish, but this time when she left the port on 4 June there were

no absentees. After a bleak voyage through the South Atlantic she crossed the equator again and made a short stop in Gibraltar bay. On Monday 17 June the Buccaneers, Sea Vixens and Gannets were flown off to their respective stations and next morning, as the *Eagle* steamed off the coast of Cornwall, 820 Squadron left the ship for Culdrose. Later that same day, after Customs formalities had been completed, the *Eagle* steamed with full ceremony through Plymouth Sound and the Hamoaze to her berth in the dockyard, where a vast crowd of family and friends were waiting to greet her. The carrier had been away from home for 308 days, and of those 220 had been spent at sea.

Although her foreign service was over, the commission was not, and after the ship's company had taken the leave which was due to them, *Eagle* was prepared for sea again. It was on Friday 23 August 1968, a hot summer's day, that the *Eagle* left Devonport to take part in a NATO exercise, 'Silver Tower'. The helicopters of 820 Squadron had embarked before sailing, and as she steamed north through the Irish Sea the Sea Vixens and Gannets were landed. Finally Buccaneers were embarked off the north-east coast of Scotland before carrying out intensive flying exercises off the Moray Firth.

Once the major exercise had started, with the *Eagle* as the only strike carrier taking part, the NATO fleet steamed north where it tested Iceland's air defences and became the subject of interest for a number of Soviet trawlers and warships. The *Eagle* led a strike group, which included the USS *Springfield* and the frigate HMS *Juno*, over the Arctic Circle, which earned the ship's company both 'Crossing the Line' and 'Bluenose' certificates in the course of the same commission. During the exercise one of the *Eagle's* helicopters crashed into the sea, fortunately with no casualties, but as those on the bridge watched the seaboat approach the stricken aircraft to rescue the aircrew, it began to sink lower and lower in the water. The horrified crew were suddenly aware of the awful realization that someone had forgotten to put the bung in. Perhaps the watching

Soviet warship thought it was all part of the exercise! For ten days the *Eagle's* aircraft operated continuously as they defended the force from attacks and carried out long-range air strikes over western Europe. The final day of the exercise was marred by severe gales and there were sighs of relief when the force arrived at Rosyth for the debriefing.

After four days at Rosyth the *Eagle* left for Devonport, steaming home by way of the Pentland Firth and the Irish Sea. The squadrons were launched on Wednesday 2 October, in thick fog, with 820 Squadron departing the following day. At 4.30pm that afternoon, Thursday 3 October 1968, with the ship's company manning the flight deck and with her paying-off pennant proudly flying, the *Eagle* steamed up the Hamoaze to her berth in the dockyard where, as always, she was greeted by a host of relatives and friends.

It was the end of another successful commission and the *Eagle* had, once again, proved what a versatile and essential part of the Royal Navy she was.

A dramatic bow view of the *Eagle* at speed. *(K. Rimmer)*

Chapter Twelve

The Sixth - And Final - Commission

Following her arrival at Devonport in October 1968, the *Eagle* began a five-month refit and on Monday 25 November her new commanding officer, Captain J. D. Treacher RN, was appointed. Captain Treacher had qualified as a Fleet Air Arm pilot in 1947, going on to command 778 Squadron in 1951 and 849 Squadron in 1952-53. He had also commanded the frigate *Lowestoft* between 1964 and 1966. Despite all the speculation as to her future, the *Eagle* was recommissioned on Wednesday 5 March 1969 and the ceremony was attended by nine Admirals, seven of whom had themselves commanded the carrier.

A few days after the ceremony the Wessex helicopters of 826 Squadron embarked from Culdrose and the *Eagle* left Devonport for her work-up and flying trials. The Sea Vixens of 899 Squadron and the Gannets of 849D Flight were embarked in the Irish Sea and the *Eagle* then steamed north and round to the area of the Moray Firth where the Buccaneers of 800 Squadron were embarked and the trials were successfully completed. In May 1969 the *Eagle* was in St Brides Bay, off the Pembrokeshire coast, for the aircraft of 899 Squadron to carry out strafing exercises. However, the training schedule was unexpectedly interrupted when two youths sailed their dinghy into the target area, as a protest about aircraft noise in a tourist area. Fortunately, although the incident received a lot of publicity, it did not

seriously affect the carrier's programme and she moved to the Channel as planned in order to carry out trials of the new McDonnell Douglas Phantom F-4K aircraft.

The Phantom had originally been purchased as a shipborne general-purpose fighter to replace the Sea Vixen, and it had been envisaged that the aircraft would be operated by the *Eagle*, the *Ark Royal* and by the proposed new aircraft carrier *CVA 01*. However, with the cancellation of the latter and the announcement that the *Eagle* would not be fully converted to operate the aircraft, it was clear that the *Ark Royal*, which was undergoing a major refit at that time, would be the only Royal Navy aircraft carrier to carry a full squadron operationally.

Trials of the aircraft had begun in April 1968 at RNAS Yeovilton and in early 1969 three of the aircraft formed a squadron which was based with the Royal Naval Test Squadron at Boscombe Down. In May 1969 a Phantom from this squadron won the Transatlantic Air Race sponsored by the *Daily Mail*, with an average speed of 956 knots, a record which stood until 1974 when it was broken by a USAF SR-71 aircraft. The sea trials of the Phantom started on Monday 2 June 1969 and two aircraft, XT 857 and XT 865, were detached from Boscombe Down to the *Eagle*. The first of the two to land on the carrier's flight deck was XT 865, flown by Commander E. Hefford RN, the commanding officer of the test squadron. These initial

A very smart display on the flight deck. *(K. Rimmer)*

2 June 1969 and a McDonnell Douglas F4K Phantom is about to make the first arrested deck landing aboard a British aircraft carrier - HMS *Eagle*.

(Fleet Air Arm Museum)

121

operations were watched by 79 senior officers from the Imperial Defence College and they saw the Phantom make three 'touch and go' circuits before the final touchdown, when Commander Hefford made a perfect landing at 130 knots before being brought to a halt by the single DAX 1 arrester wire. As he taxied to his parking lot the second aircraft, piloted by Lt-Cdr R. Burn RN, landed and, apart from shredding the tyre on the port wheel, he too made a perfect landing. When interviewed by the Press representatives who were on board for the occasion, Commander Hefford commented: 'There were absolutely no problems. We have simulated this many times and in the event it was a smooth display.'

Over the following two weeks the Phantom's sea trials continued, with aircraft being launched and landed each day, and at their conclusion 61 arrested landings had been executed.

Upon completion of the Phanton trials the *Eagle* steamed west across the Atlantic to visit the US ports of Norfolk, Virginia, and Boston, Mass., both of which were very popular runs ashore. The *Eagle* arrived during the last week of June and there is no doubt that, for hospitality, the USA would take some beating. The naval base at Norfolk had a PX that would put many department stores to shame, and within easy reach of the *Eagle's* berth there were also clubs, a theatre and even a 'WAVES' barracks. Also very popular were visits to Virginia Beach and coach trips to Washington DC. The deployment to the USA ended with the visit to Boston, which was equally as enjoyable as Norfolk. During the stay the ship's Padres worked tirelessly, organizing coach trips to various tourist destinations, including the city of New York.

Following her return to UK waters the *Eagle* was the flagship of Admiral Sir John Bush KCB DSC, C-in-C Western Fleet, at the Royal Review of the Western Fleet in Torbay. The Review started on Monday 28 July when the Queen and the Duke of Edinburgh, accompanied by the Prince of Wales and Princess Anne, travelled by train from London to Torquay where they embarked in the Royal Yacht, *Britannia*. That afternoon the royal party visited a number of ships of the fleet and in the evening they attended a dinner aboard the *Eagle*, hosted by the C-in-C, before attending a fleet concert in the *Eagle's* hangar. Later that night the wind got up and returning the royal party to *Britannia*, and getting the sailors and Wrens back to their ships or ashore proved to be very tricky. Nevertheless, despite the difficulties, the evening was a great success.

Next morning, with the strong winds still blowing, the presentation of new Colours to the fleet was held in the *Eagle's* hangar, instead of on the flight deck as had been originally intended, and once again choppy seas meant a difficult transfer from *Britannia* to *Eagle*. After the presentation Her Majesty addressed the Parade, and Admiral Sir John Bush replied. Following his speech there

Phantom XT 865 piloted by Commander E. Hefford makes naval aviation history as it catches the arrester wire for a perfect landing. *(Fleet Air Arm Museum)*

was a fly-past by 89 Fleet Air Arm aircraft, starting with Wessex helicopters flying at a height of only 400ft and at a leisurely 80 knots, and ending with the Phantoms which roared overhead at 800ft and at a speed of 360 knots.

That afternoon all the ships put to sea where, ten miles off the coast of Devon, they staged a very impressive steam-past. The *Eagle* led the Review of the Western Fleet as her ship's company manned and cheered ship, and she was followed by the newly converted, but rather ungainly looking, helicopter cruiser HMS *Blake*. Next came the guided missile destroyer HMS *Hampshire* and 12 frigates, before the *Britannia* steamed in the opposite direction to take the salutes of the second column led by HMS *Glamorgan*, which was followed by the nuclear submarines *Valiant* and *Warspite*, six conventional submarines, and an array of minesweepers and Royal Fleet Auxiliaries.

At the conclusion of the Review the Duke of Edinburgh and the Prince of Wales left HMS *Blake* by helicopter, while the Queen and Princess Anne disembarked from

A Phantom F4K on the catapult. *(Fleet Air Arm Museum)*

Britannia and left Torquay by train. It had been a successful two days and it was the last occasion on which the Queen's Colour was presented to the fleet.

A few days later, before the summer leave period, a 'Families Day' was held on board the *Eagle*, with all the guests embarking whilst the ship was moored to C buoy in Plymouth Sound. The carrier then steamed out to Lyme Bay where the visitors were treated to a full flying display, after which the ship steamed back to Devonport while the families enjoyed a special performance by the concert party. The general consensus was that it had been an excellent day.

In the autumn of 1969, after the summer leave had been taken, the *Eagle* left Devonport for the Mediterranean where she took part in a NATO exercise, and visited Gibraltar, Malta, Naples and Toulon. During the visit to Naples the Roman Catholic Padre organized what became known as 'Rosary Tours' to Rome which proved to be very popular. While in the port the ship was open to visitors who could, of course, go on board free of charge. As usual the *Eagle* drew a good crowd, but during the afternoon some young 'urchins' from the city were found to be selling

'tickets' to members of the public, and they were doing very well out of it! The *Eagle* had gone into Naples straight after the NATO exercise and because of her deep draught there was only one berth available at which she could go alongside. As she was not able to fuel beforehand she went alongside light, with only 4,000 tons of furnace fuel oil in her tanks. It was, therefore, critical that she should refuel from RFA *Olna* as soon as she left the port and without any delay. However, on sailing day, the master of the *Olna* contacted Captain Treacher and informed him that one of the key members of his ship's company had been invloved in a fracas ashore and had been arrested by the local police, who would not release him. As the *Eagle* had only enough fuel to get her out of harbour this was a real problem, and Captain Treacher spent most of the last day in the port working with the British Consul to get the man released. Fortunately, the police let the man go only hours before the ships were due to sail.

In October the *Eagle* took part in exercises in the Aegean Sea, and on Trafalgar Day Captain Treacher presented the captain of the shadowing Soviet Petya-class frigate with a

The *Eagle* dressed overall and moored at C buoy in Plymouth Sound in June 1969. Fort Picklecombe can be seen on the shore of Cawsand Bay.
(K. Rimmer)

bottle of whisky. One of the carrier's Wessex helicopters flew over the Soviet vessel and a crew member was winched down bearing the bottle. The captain of the Russian vessel picked up the whisky and, in the words of the Ministry of Defence, 'The Russians waved them goodbye with their glasses.'

In November 1969, just before Christmas leave, the *Eagle* took part in 'Exercise Decamp' in the Atlantic with HMS *Hermes*. In early 1970 she was involved in exercises in the Moray Firth area and later she made a goodwill visit to Liverpool before, on Wednesday 25 March, she returned to Devonport for a six months' Docking and Essential Defects (DED) period.

In April, following the seasonal leave periods, the ship's company moved on board HMS *Centaur* which had been towed round from Portsmouth to provide accommodation whilst the *Eagle* was in No 10 dry dock. On Tuesday 2 June 1970 there was a change of command when Captain Treacher was relieved by Captain I. G. W. Robertson DSC RN, who was to be her last commanding officer. Captain Robertson had qualified as a pilot during the Second World War and he had carried out air strikes on enemy shipping and attacks on the German battleship *Tirpitz*, for which he was awarded the DSC. In the early 1960s he had commanded the frigates *Keppel* and *Mohawk* and he had also been the commanding officer of RNAS Culdrose.

During that month the Conservative Party won the

General Election, but it soon became clear that there was to be no reversal of the decision to withdraw the *Eagle* from operational service, and that she was now on her final commission.

When the time came for *Eagle* to be refloated and moved out to the tidal berth once again there was relief all round as everyone could move back on board to the comparative comfort of 'home'. It was during the afternoon of Saturday 26 September that the *Eagle* left Devonport once again and the squadrons rejoined her. Over the following two weeks the ship was put through her paces and everyone found their sea legs. On the morning of Friday 9 October, as the *Eagle* was returning to her berth at Devonport for a short rectification period, she touched rocks some 100 yards offshore in Plymouth Sound which meant that she had to be dry docked once again. The incident happened at about 11.15am as the carrier rounded Smeaton Pass, between West Hoe Terrace and Drake's Island, and the vibration was felt in B and Y engine rooms as several blades on their respective propellers were damaged. Before the *Eagle* could get back into the dry dock however, the *Bulwark* had to be temporarily moved out. Once the repairs could get under way, the starboard after propeller was exchanged for a three-bladed version, and some damaged hull plating was made good. Finally, on Monday 9 November, the *Eagle* put to sea once again

The *Eagle* alongside her berth in Devonport Dockyard in the autumn of 1969. She was a familiar sight for the thousands of tourists who visited the city.

(J. A. Slater)

Sardinia, before putting into Malta for a short self-maintenance period. She left Malta on Monday 22 March, and after calling in at Gibraltar for a brief visit on the way home, she arrived in Plymouth Sound on Wednesday 7 April. After clearing HM Customs during the forenoon, families were embarked and the *Eagle* steamed up the Hamoaze to her berth in the dockyard. It was a poignant reunion for the ship's company and their families, as a postal strike had caused a virtual blackout of news in both directions during the whole trip.

During her stay in Devonport, as well as the taking of seasonal leave, which went all too quickly, the ship was loaded with all types of stores. The withdrawal from the Singapore Naval Base was scheduled for the end of October that year and the *Eagle* had to embark everything which might be needed for her eight-month deployment on the Far East Station. She made her last operational departure from Devonport on Wednesday 26 May and, after embarking the aircraft in the Bristol Channel, she set courses for Cape Town on 1 June.

As she steamed south, in company with the destroyer HMS *Glamorgan* and the under way replenishment group, *Reliant*, *Resource* and *Tidepool*, the carrier passed close to the Canary Islands. Later in the passage a day was set aside for the 'Crossing the Line' ceremony when, with a full court of 'policemen', 'mermaids', and 'bears', the first person to be ducked was Captain Robertson, swiftly followed by the Commander, Surgeon, Dentist, 'Schooly' and the youngest member of the ship's company. Then, with the formal duckings over, many unprepared spectators were also thrown unceremoniously into the improvised canvas pool. When flying operations permitted, the flight deck became a hive of activity with keep-fit enthusiasts running, doing press-ups and holding deck hockey tournaments, while the gamblers held 'race meetings' organizing themselves into bookies and punters.

With Ascension Island available as a diversion runway, the aircraft took over the flight deck once again and sports teams were landed on the island. As the *Eagle* steamed still further south, the ship's company changed back into blues for the southern hemisphere's winter and once they were off Cape Town, FO2 FES, Rear-Admiral D. J. Williams, embarked by helicopter and hoisted his flag in the *Eagle*.

During the stay in Cape Town everyone had an

and courses were set for the Moray Firth area where the ship's flying trials were to be carried out.

One major change which was noticed when the squadrons re-embarked were the helicopters of 826 Squadron, as the Wessex Mk IIIs had been exchanged for Sea Kings, which had already proved themselves when the master of a Greek vessel had been lifted from his ship off Penzance and taken to hospital ashore. On Friday 13 November a Sea Vixen of 899 Squadron crashed into the sea after being launched from the bow catapult, but fortunately the aircrew were rescued by the ship's SAR Flight, although one member of the crew suffered back injuries. On Saturday 21 November the *Eagle* made a goodwill visit to Southampton, where she went alongside 107 berth in the port's Western Docks. This berth was usually used by P&O's liners *Canberra* and *Oriana*, but the *Eagle* proved just as popular in the port and when she was opened to the public the next day queues of people stretched for over half a mile down Herbert Walker Avenue, with the total number of visitors amounting to more than 4,500. After a successful six-day stay the *Eagle* sailed for the Bristol Channel where she carried out exercises with the frigates *Chichester* and *Danae*, before returning to Devonport on Thursday 10 December for Christmas and New Year leave.

On Tuesday 19 January 1971 the *Eagle* left Devonport, this time setting course for Gibraltar where she was to carry out her third work-up and undergo her Operational Readiness Inspection. This was carried out by Rear-Admiral J. D. Treacher who, having commanded the ship during the first leg of the commission, had an intimate knowledge of the carrier. Admiral Treacher was impressed with the ship and she passed the inspection with flying colours which allowed for some relaxation, and this was taken at the Riviera resort of Villefranche where *Eagle* anchored on 12 February. After leaving the Cote d' Azur the carrier took part in 'Exercise Perfect Princess' off

Full-power trials in September 1970. *(Fleet Air Arm Museum)*

The *Eagle* leaving Naples with Mount Vesuvius in the background. *(K. Rimmer)*

opportunity to experience the tremendous hospitality for which the city is renowned, and there were more than a few bleary eyes when the ship sailed for Singapore on Tuesday 22 June, after five hectic days. Whilst the carrier was off Mauritius the squadrons staged a fly-past and flying display for the residents of St Louis, and on Thursday 8 July the *Eagle* arrived at Singapore's Naval Base for a 13-day assisted maintenance period. Despite the swimming pools and the bright lights of Singapore city there were few regrets when, on 21 July, the *Eagle* sailed for a series of goodwill visits to Australian and New Zealand ports. After leaving, a day was spent navigating close to the coast so that the aircraft could re-embark from RAF Tengah, before *Eagle* set courses south and east for the Sunda Strait between Sumatra and Java, bound for the waters of the Indian Ocean off the city of Perth, Western Australia.

However, as she was steaming through the Java Sea, a serious fire broke out in one of the ship's liquid oxygen plants which was potentially extremely dangerous, and the entire ship went to emergency stations. With most of the ship's company, apart from those required to steam the ship, mustered on the flight deck, it took fire parties about two hours to extinguish the blaze. Two men who were working in the compartment at the time were injured in the initial explosion, and the *Eagle* returned to the waters off Singapore so that they could be flown to the British Military Hospital on the island. Sadly, one of the men, MEA J. Laity, died two weeks later from his injuries. The resulting fire damage was confined to the oxygen plant and

the dental surgery directly above it, which was gutted.

As the ship's operational efficiency was not affected by the fire, it was not long before the *Eagle* arrived off the Australian coast. On completion of exercises there, the carrier steamed across the Great Australian Bight and round to the east coast, where on the morning of Wednesday 4 August she passed the Heads and entered Sydney Harbour.

Whilst at Sydney the Sea Vixens and Buccaneers provided a fly-past over the city, and an 18-year-old nurse, Miss Elizabeth McCracken, was invited on board. She was, of course, the girl born on board the *Eagle* on 15 June 1953, during the *Eagle's* first commission when she was present at the Coronation Review. As soon as Captain Robertson knew that *Eagle* would be visiting Sydney, he had sent Elizabeth a telegram, promising to bring her birthplace to her in Australia. After being shown round the ship she was presented with a small gift and the youngest member of the ship's company, JMEM F. Slattery, presented her with a bouquet of flowers.

When *Eagle* left Sydney on Monday 9 August severe weather forced the cancellation of plans to steam through the Cook Strait to participate in exercises east of New Zealand, and *Eagle*, together with her escorts *Glamorgan*, *Danae*, *Achilles*, *Jaguar*, HMAS *Ovens*, HMNZS *Waikato* and *Wirangi*, was forced to ride out the storms. Fortunately, when the weather improved the scheduled visit to Wellington was able to go ahead. Five days later the *Eagle* headed west for Fremantle, the port for Perth at the

During her stay in Southampton during 1970, the *Eagle* was as popular as the P&O liners which normally used the berth.

(*Southern Daily Echo, Southampton*)

Eagle's arrival at Villefranche on 12 February 1971.

(*Fleet Air Arm Museum*)

The *Eagle* arrives in Malta's Grand Harbour on 4 March 1971. HMS *Norfolk* is in the foreground. *(M. Cassar)*

A Sea Hawk makes an emergency landing into the crash barrier...

...and is successfully brought to a rest as firefighters and emergency teams rush to rescue the aircrew. *(P. Horan)*

A Gannet is prepared for launching.
(P. Horan)

As the *Eagle* steamed south to Cape Town she really did 'Cross the Line'. In this view she was off Ascension Island. *(P. Horan)*

The *Eagle* enters Sydney Harbour early on the morning of 4 August 1971.
(P. Horan)

...a Buccaneer on the catapult. *(P. Horan)*

A Sea Vixen lands on and...

mouth of the Swan River. On the first night of the stay the city put on a ship's dance at the Perth Ballroom, during which the beer was sold in gallon jugs and a 'Miss *Eagle*' was chosen. An adventurous group of the ship's company went on an 'exped' with a lorry and a minibus lent by the Australian Navy, to the Peel Inlet, 50 miles south of Perth. It was on Tuesday 14 September that the *Eagle* bade a final goodbye to Australia and at least 50 cars lined up on the mole to wish the carrier a noisy farewell.

When the *Eagle* returned to the Singapore Naval Base she passed HMS *Albion* which was leaving for Subic Bay and Hong Kong. In the Naval Base itself there were unmistakeable signs that the withdrawal was well under way,

and at a short ceremony there the Far East Colour was paraded and transferred to the *Eagle* for the passage to Portsmouth. The Colour, which was one of two remaining for sea commands, represented the Queen on the Far East Station. The second was the Western Fleet Colour, which replaced the Home Fleet Colour, and which had been presented by the Queen in Torbay earlier in the commission.

After sailing from Singapore the *Eagle* steamed to an exercise area west of Subic Bay, but as there were three typhoons in the region at the time it was difficult to find an area where the weather was suitable for flying operations. It was during this period, at 2.45pm on Friday 8 October, that an SOS was received from the US-

registered merchant ship, SS *Steel Vendor*, which had gone aground on a reef off an unmarked island, Loai Ta, in the South China Sea. The merchantman had been en route from Manila to Saigon with a cargo of 10,000 tons of cement when she developed engine trouble, which left her drifting for two days. Despite the fact that weather conditions had caused flying operations to be cancelled, two Sea Kings were successfully launched in the most hazardous conditions, when the *Eagle* was 60 miles away from the stricken ship. At just after 4pm the helicopters located the *Steel Vendor*, which was well and truly stuck on the reef, and one of the aircrew was lowered by winch. This was another dangerous operation with strong winds blowing, and the fact that the lowering rope had to be longer than the aircrew would have liked, in order to keep the helicopter clear of the ship's masts and derrick posts. The master of the *Steel Vendor*, Captain Lambert, quickly accepted the offer of assistance and two more helicopters were launched in order to evacuate the 40 crew members. At the same time, on board *Eagle*, emergency packs were broken out, camp beds rigged up, fresh clothes were set out and hot meals were prepared. Fortunately, before dusk, all the *Steel Vendor's* crew had been evacuated and next day they were flown to Cubi Point, an airfield near Manila, where they were safely landed just 24 hours after their SOS was received.

Shortly afterwards two messages of appreciation were received on board *Eagle*. The first read: 'Captain Robertson - CO *Eagle* - wish to convey to you our heartfelt thanks and admiration for the magnificent performance of your officers, crew and aircraft in rescue of entire crew of *Steel Vendor* on 8 October 1971. Mercer, President, Ithmian Lines.' The second signal was from the Commander, US Naval Forces, Philippines, Rear-Admiral G. R. Muse, and it read: 'Your rescue of the crew of SS *Steel Vendor* was noted with great pleasure. The professional manner in which the rescue was effected, the care afforded the survivors while on board, your fine communications and the efficiency demonstrated in putting the survivors ashore was most noteworthy and should be a source of pride to all concerned. Please convey my sincere appreciation and well done to all hands.'

Following the conclusion of exercises off the Philippines, the *Eagle* set course for Hong Kong where she arrived on Friday 15 October for a short maintenance period. During the stay Jenny's Side Party painted the ship's hull and a Ceremonial Guard paraded at a service to mark the retirement of the Governor. Shortly before the *Eagle* left Hong Kong, Princess Anne visited the colony and to mark the event the ship's aircraft, which were at Kai Tak, provided a fly-past and the *Eagle* fired a 21-gun salute. The ship's wardroom was chosen as the venue for HMS *Tamar's* Trafalgar Day Dinner, and for the occasion the Queen's Far East Colour was displayed behind the top table.

After leaving Hong Kong the *Eagle* steamed back to Singapore territorial waters where her aircraft performed a fly-past to mark the final British withdrawal from the island base, before the carrier joined *Albion*, *Glamorgan*, *Scylla*, *Arethusa*, *Achilles*, *Argonaut*, *Ghurka*, and Australian and New Zealand units for 'Exercise Curtain Call' in the Malacca Strait. During the exercise the entire fleet anchored off Langkowi Island where a huge barbeque and a fleet 'It's A Knockout' contest were held.

From the Penang area the *Eagle* steamed back across the Indian Ocean to Gan for flying exercises, and then north-west into the Arabian Sea and to the waters off Masirah

A Royal Australian Navy A4 Skyhawk being launched from the *Eagle*...

...and an S2F Tracker.
(*P. Horan*)

The *Eagle* arrives at Fremantle, Western Australia.
(*P. Horan*)

HMS *Eagle*, the Navy's biggest warship. *(K. Rimmer)*

from where she was to provide air cover for the British withdrawal from the Persian Gulf. There then followed eight weeks at sea which, although not a record, was extremely trying in the searing heat. During this period the aircraft were able to spend a great deal of time carrying out flying practice, using RAF Masirah as the diversion airfield. It was at this time that the Under Secretary of State for the Navy announced that *Eagle* was to be scrapped on completion of the commission. On board the carrier, however, life went on as usual with 'beard growing' competitions, soapbox orators, sports tournaments and practical jokes. A planned visit to Mombasa was cancelled and it was thought that the *Eagle* would accompany the *Albion* to stand by in the Bay of Bengal in case assistance was required by British subjects caught up in the war between India and Pakistan, which eventually resulted in the establishment of Bangladesh. However, as the *Albion* steamed east, the *Eagle* was required only to transfer stores and four of 826 Squadron's Sea Kings to the commando ship.

As the *Albion*, complete with a large Union Flag painted on her flight deck, left the Arabian Sea the *Eagle* set courses for East Africa where, off Mombasa, FO2 FES was transferred by helicopter to the *Triumph*, which was moored in Kilindini Harbour, and the *Eagle* continued on to Durban where she arrived on Wednesday 22 December, having spent 56 days at sea. The carrier tied up alongside a

quay on the southern side of the large harbour complex which entailed a long haul to get to the other side, but with the help of the ship's boats and a charter firm, the journey was made much easier.

Soon after her arrival, Christmas decorations began to adorn the mess decks, with a Star of David on the main radar aerial which was lit at night. The people of Durban, renowned for their hospitality, shared their time and their homes with the *Eagle's* ship's company and for most it was a Christmas and New Year to remember. However, for those who preferred to entertain themselves there were beaches and a host of other attractions, including trips to game reserves and to scenic areas of the country. The *Eagle's* shipwrights built a splendid Wendy house for one of the city's orphanages, and when the ship was opened to visitors for two days, over 20,000 came to look round. At one time one of the gangways collapsed, because it was so overloaded with people. Fortunately, there were no serious injuries and one member of the ship's company went over the side immediately to assist those who had fallen in the water. Christmas Day on board was marked by carol services and hymn singing while the New Year was seen in with 16 bells being rung, and for the first ten minutes of 1972 the harbour was a cacophony of noise with all the ships sounding their sirens and flashing their lights. The *Eagle's* large spotlights illuminated some apartments

The *Eagle* at speed. *(P. Horan)*

HMS *Eagle* enters Durban harbour. This was her last foreign visit but, as always, both the carrier and her ship's company present a splendid sight. *(K. Rimmer)*

Replenishment at Sea. *Eagle* with the RFAs *Olna* (A123) and *Resource* (A480). *(P. Horan)*

On 8 October 1971 the *Eagle* answered an SOS call from the SS *Steel Vendor* which was aground on an unmarked reef in the South China Sea. Here, in very hazardous conditions, one of the carrier's Sea Kings winches members of her crew to safety. *(P. Horan)*

A small group of well-wishers brave the rain and cold to watch the *Eagle* arrive at Portsmouth on the morning of Wednesday 26 January 1972. She is flying her paying-off pennant and the flag of Rear-Admiral J. D. Treacher. *(Fleet Air Arm Museum)*

A very smart arrival at Hong Kong on Friday 15 October 1971 and...

137

...an equally immaculate departure. *(K. Rimmer)*

opposite her berth, and the residents replied enthusiastically by flashing their room lights.

During the stay in the port the four Sea Kings which had transferred to *Albion* returned 'home' as the commando ship passed by Durban, on her way to Cape Town. The *Eagle* left Durban on the morning of Tuesday 4 January 1972 and, apart from slowing down off Simonstown to pick up mail, she steamed non-stop to Gibraltar which she had been ordered to make at her best speed, and to stand by to make a fast passage to Malta, where British troops were withdrawing from the island. The prospect of a further stint in the Mediterranean was most unpopular but, fortunately, it was not necessary, and after spending the night of 19 January in Gibraltar Bay, *Eagle* weighed anchor for the final leg of the deployment as courses were set for Portsmouth.

For some months Heads of Department had been preparing plans for the removal of stores, equipment and ammunition, and the squadron's ground crews had been working hard to ensure that all the aircraft were serviceable. In keeping with the times, 'flower power' motifs were appearing on the aircraft, together with a few rude messages. All the fixed-wing aircraft and the helicopters were launched on 22 and 23 January and 826 Squadron's Sea Kings flew off as well, leaving only one Buccaneer without an engine on board. The last fixed-wing launch was reserved for a model triplane followed by a scale model of the ship, dubbed 'Little E'.

The *Eagle* herself anchored off Spithead on the morning of Tuesday 25 January and HM Customs were embarked. As the *Eagle* lay at anchor that night strong winds started to blow and for a while there was a real possibility that she would not be able to enter harbour as planned. Fortunately, although Wednesday 26 January 1972 dawned as a wet and dull day, the *Eagle* was able to weigh anchor at 7.30am and, with the ship's company manning a very wet flight deck, make her way into Portsmouth Harbour. Not only was she flying the flag of Flag Officer Aircraft Carriers & Amphibious Ships, Rear-Admiral J. D. Treacher, she was

also flying her 450ft-long paying-off pennant. Special dispensation had been granted for this privilege as, according to Queen's Regulations, an Admiral's flag has priority over masthead or paying-off pennants. As she steamed past Southsea seafront hundreds of people defied the cold and rain to bid farewell to a 'grand old lady'. Unfortunately, weather conditions caused the cancellation of a fly-past salute by her squadrons, but as she reached the harbour entrance crowds stood on the Round Tower waving and cheering as she passed slowly by, looking as immaculate as ever. She had steamed some 74,000 miles and had received a tremendous welcome in each port she had visited. As soon as she was secured alongside in Portsmouth Dockyard, and the brows were in place, over 3,000 relatives and friends poured on board for their long-awaited reunion. Captain Robertson, when interviewed by the Press, was philosophical in his reply: 'This is a sad day for me and the ship's company, but there is no room for sentimentality. We have achieved the task we set out to perform eight months ago and I believe we have done it well. When it is known that a ship is being scrapped it is difficult to maintain dynamism, but the ship has been busier than in any previous commission.'

Shortly after *Eagle* berthed, the C-in-C Fleet, Admiral Sir Edward Ashmore, embarked to present commendations to four members of the ship's company who were involved in fighting the fire in the oxygen plant in June the previous year. By early afternoon most of the ship's company had dispersed on leave and to new drafts. That evening Captain Robertson held a small dinner party for four of his predecessors and their wives; Vice-Admiral L. D. Empson (Second Sea Lord) and Mrs Empson; Vice-Admiral Sir John Roxburgh (Flag Officer Submarines) and Lady Roxburgh; Rear-Admiral J. E. Pope (Chief of Staff C-in-C Fleet) and Mrs Pope, and Rear-Admiral J. D. Treacher (Flag Officer Aircraft Carriers & Amphibious Ships) and Mrs Treacher.

The *Eagle's* final commission was over, but controversy surrounding her demise raged on.

The *Eagle* is berthed alongside for the last time. *(Fleet Air Arm Museum)*

Chapter Thirteen

The Sad Demise Of A Proud Ship

The task of destoring, de-ammunitioning and de-equipping started on the day after the *Eagle's* arrival in Portsmouth and during March 1972 it was made easier by the construction of a large, hinged road bridge over which three-ton trucks could drive from the quayside and onto the flight deck. As the *Eagle's* draught was lightened and she rose higher and higher in the water, the controversy regarding her early withdrawal and, in fact, the demise of the Navy's fixed-wing capability, raged on both in the Press and in Parliament.

Opponents of the proposal to phase out the Navy's fixed-wing aircraft carriers, which had been dubbed 'Healey's Hatchet', had hoped for at least a partial reversal of the decision from Edward Heath's Conservative Government. However, they were only appeased a little by the decision to keep the *Ark Royal* in service until the late 1970s, despite the fact that the *Eagle's* electronic warfare and radar capability was far superior. Only £5 million would have been required to make the *Eagle* fully capable of operating Phantom aircraft and then she and the *Ark Royal* would have constituted a formidable force together, acting as a great deterrent. Another very valid concern was the fact that the first of a new generation of aircraft carriers, or 'through deck cruisers' as they were known at that time, which had been designed specifically to operate Sea Harriers, would not be fully operational

until mid-1980 and there would be a serious gap in Britain's defences between the demise of *Ark Royal* and the introduction of the new ships.

But all the arguments in *Eagle's* favour were to no avail and it was announced that: 'The possibility of putting the ship into reserve has been examined, but it has been concluded that she should be disposed of by scrapping.' There was to be no last minute reprieve for the *Eagle*. It was clear that the Conservative Government, with its eyes firmly fixed on Europe, had no more intention of saving the Fleet Air Arm from decimation than had the previous Labour administration.

Meanwhile, on board the *Eagle* at Portsmouth, the job of removing all the ship's heavy equipment was making rapid progress as a steady stream of fully laden trucks drove down from the flight deck. As late as March 1972, the future of the *Eagle* was being debated in the House of Lords where the Secretary of State for Defence, Lord Carrington, was asked whether, in view of the strong support for retaining HMS *Eagle* in maintained reserve, the Government would change its mind about scrapping the ship. The question, which was asked by Lord Ewing, was supported by other members of the Upper House, with only one dissenter, Lord Shinwell, who was entirely predictable when he remarked: 'The move to stop HMS *Eagle* going to the scrapyard is largely emotional', thus failing to appreciate what use she would be. Lord Carrington was uncompromising when he replied: 'It is always sad when a ship reaches the end of her life, the more so when her passing is felt in some respects to mark the passing of an era. The limitations of a single aircraft carrier are obvious. You must regard HMS *Ark Royal* as a contribution to NATO naval forces. Her deployment and refits will, as far as possible, be coordinated with Britain's allies. After a thorough and careful study the

HMS *Eagle* as she leaves Portsmouth under tow for her lay-up berth at Devonport.
(Maritime Photo Library)

The *Eagle* is towed from Portsmouth on Wednesday 9 August 1972. The smoke from her funnel was caused by a flare which had been set off just for show.

(*The News, Portsmouth*)

The *Eagle* laid up off Cremyll where she remained from August 1972 until October 1978.   *(M. Cassar)*

Government came to the conclusion that it was not practicable to run HMS *Eagle* on after 1972. If I had a lot more money available I would not seek to keep HMS *Eagle* in commission, but would seek to speed up the entry into service of the new weapons. The arguments against keeping the vessel in reserve are conclusive. Initially, she would need a refit costing between £2 million and £4 million and frequent refits afterwards. Even under the most favourable circumstances, it would take four and a half months to get her out of reserve and made fully operational.' He ended his reply by stating: 'HMS *Eagle* will be towed to Devonport later this year where certain items of her equipment will be earmarked for *Ark Royal*. A decision on when she will be disposed of as scrap probably will not be taken before the end of 1973. If circumstances change between now and 1973 the Government could have another look at the matter, but I do not see how they could have ever come to any other decision.' Clearly, there was absolutely no political will at all to retain the *Eagle,* even in reserve.

By the summer of 1972 the *Eagle's* compartments had almost been stripped bare of reusable equipment and on Wednesday 9 August she left Portsmouth for the last time as three large ocean-going tugs towed the helpless hulk out through the harbour entrance and into the Solent, bound for Devonport. Once again hundreds of people turned out to wave farewell, among them crowds of holidaymakers who were staying in Southsea. There was not much glory left for the carrier, and the burst of smoke from her funnel as she left harbour came from a flare which had been put on for show. Across her stern there was a large banner proclaiming, 'Goodbye Beautiful'.

The tow down the Channel took two days and it was late afternoon on Friday 11 August when she was brought through Plymouth Sound, with darkness falling as she was manoeuvred to her lay-up mooring off Cremyll, at the entrance to Millbrook Lake. Over the next few weeks hundreds of nostalgic and inquisitive visitors came to look at the old ship and, for a time, her presence boosted the number of passengers using the Cremyll Ferry. The 'Big

E', with Mount Edgcumbe as a backdrop, provided a spectacular sight for tourists crossing the Hamoaze.

For over six years the *Eagle* lay at the mooring off Cremyll and, as the months and years slipped by, her presence there became less and less of a tourist attraction. Over the years she was continually plundered as she provided spares for the *Ark Royal*. Finally, on Monday 4 September 1978, it was announced that the ship had been sold for scrap. She had been purchased for £1½ million by Steel Supply Company (Western) Ltd, who had leased a pier facility at Cairnryan in Scotland from the Loch Ryan Harbour Company. The buyers were actually based in Swansea and the purchase price reflected the high scrap metal prices at that time.

The *Eagle* left Devonport for the last time on Friday 13 October, just eight days before Trafalgar Day, when six tugs shepherded the carrier from the Hamoaze into Plymouth Sound. It was the *Eagle's* final departure from her home base and it was a bright, sunny day as she was moved slowly out of the harbour. This time there was no ship's company to man her flight deck, no Royal Marines Band and no gun salute to the Flag Officer Plymouth, as she was towed past silent crowds who lined the vantage points from the dockyard to Devil's Point on one side, and Cremyll on the other side. The large numbers who turned out were evidence of the proud affection in which the *Eagle*, once the Navy's mightiest warship, was held by the people of Plymouth and the surrounding area.

When she reached Jennycliff Bay she was halted as the three ocean-going tugs, *Rollicker, Roysterer* and *Robust*, took over the tow and a helicopter hovered over her flight deck once again as the working party who had changed the tow were winched up on completion of their task. Darkness was falling as the carrier was towed past the breakwater and she disappeared into a thick fog which had rolled in to shroud the area. As the funereal procession made its way slowly northwards through the Irish Sea, weather conditions deteriorated and the three tugs and their charge had to shelter off the Irish coast. On Monday 16 October, the day that the *Eagle* had been due to arrive at Cairnryan, it was found that the carrier and her trio of tugs had drifted south from Belfast Lough where, ironically, they had tried to take shelter, to a position about 20 miles south of Strangford Lough. Next day, although the wind had abated, it was still blowing far too hard to consider berthing her and during the afternoon the tugs struggled to

The *Eagle's* final resting place at Cairnryan. This photograph was taken just three days after her arrival at the scrapyard. (*I. Johnston*)

Looking sad and neglected the *Eagle* lies alongside the deep water wharf at Cairnryan. On 31 December 1978 the old carrier made one last bid for freedom when her forward moorings broke in an easterly gale. It was three days before she was secured alongside once again.

(*I. Johnston*)

145

The once immaculate quarterdeck awaits the cutting torches...

...as does the angled flight deck.
(I. Johnston)

keep the *Eagle* on course, about 20 miles south-west of the Mull of Galloway.

By the morning of Wednesday 18 October she was only a short distance from the mouth of Loch Ryan, but the old carrier was not giving up without a good fight, and as she was manoeuvred near the Milleur Buoy at the entrance to the loch, one of the tow ropes snapped. As the *Eagle* was towed into the loch by the two remaining tugs, and when she was about 300 yards offshore from the South deep, her bow suddenly veered to port and stuck fast on a sandbank. The tugs were unable to pull her off and with the tide ebbing, attempts to refloat her were abandoned. The next high tide was at 2am on Thursday 19 October, and it was then that the tugs managed to slide her off the sandbar. So, in a blaze of floodlights, the *Eagle* was finally secured, port side to, alongside the deep water wharf at Cairnryan, which had been constructed as berths for ocean-going ships during the dark days of the Second World War, after the fall of France, when south coast ports were untenable.

It had been intended that the demolition of the *Eagle* would begin just before the end of 1978. The contract was with Deans Marine, a family business based in Kent, and it would provide work for up to 30 men for just over two years. But still the *Eagle* was not going to give up easily and on the last day of December 1978, before the shipbreaking operations had really got under way, severe storms blew up in the area with easterly gales buffeting the loch. During the early hours of Sunday 31 December the strong winds broke the *Eagle's* forward moorings, and the ship started to move away from the jetty until she was lying at right angles to it, with only two thin steel hawsers securing her stern. Fortunately, these held firm and further lines were soon passed across to avert the immediate danger of her breaking free. As it was, the bow of the carrier was left jutting out into the deep water channel which was used by the Stranraer to Larne ferry. The *Eagle* was finally pushed back into her berth on Thursday 4 January 1979 and four days later demolition began in earnest.

By the time the last of the Navy's big carriers, *Ark Royal*, arrived at Cairnryan in September 1980, to meet the same fate, what was left of the *Eagle* had been beached in a depression, which had been scooped out by mechanical diggers, with shingle pressed around the hulk. This had caused her back to break, allowing oil and sludge to spill out of her double bottom. Soon after this she had ceased to exist.

And so ended the career of one of the most powerful warships the Royal Navy had ever possessed. She had also been one of the happiest and most efficient, serving the country well.

'Finis'.

Appendix One

Principal Particulars (As Built)

Length Overall:		804ft
Beam Overall:		135ft
Standard Displacement	1951:	36,800 tons
	1957:	43,340 tons
	1964:	54,100 tons
Draught:		33ft
Armament:		16 twin 4.5in
		8 sextuple/2 twin/9 single 40mm Bofors
Aircraft:		65
Main Propulsion Machinery:		Quadruple screw: Four sets Parsons single-reduction geared turbines. Steam provided by eight Admiralty Three Drum Boilers in four boiler rooms
SHP:		152,000
Speed:		31 knots
Complement (with embarked squadrons):		2,500
Flight Deck	1951:	Standard axial deck
	1954:	$5^{1}/_{2}°$ partial angled flight deck
	1964:	$8^{1}/_{2}°$ angled flight deck Two aircraft lifts
Deck Recognition Letter:		J (1951-1957) E (1958-1972)
Pennant Number:		RO5

Appendix Two

Commanding Officers HMS *Eagle*

	Date Appointed.
Captain G. Willoughby RN	7.3.51
Captain A. N. C. Bingley OBE RN	9.11.52
Captain D. E. Holland-Martin DSO DSC RN	28.12.53
Captain E. D. G. Lewin CBE DSO DSC RN	18.1.55
Captain H. C. D. MacLean DSC RN	30.1.56
Captain M. Le Fanu DSC RN	18.2.57
Captain J. B. Frewen RN	15.2.58
Captain L. D. Empson RN	3.12.63
Captain J. C. Y. Roxburgh DSO DSC* RN	20.7.65
Captain J. E. Pope RN	4.5.67
Captain J. D. Treacher RN	25.11.68
Captain I. G. W. Robertson DSC RN	2.6.70

Appendix Three

Former *Eagles*

The name *Eagle* appears in naval records of Queen Elizabeth I's reign. In 1592, four years after the defeat of the Spanish Armada, the *Eagle of Lubeck* (894 tons) was purchased from the Hanseatic League for £70 and used as a hulk for the storage of ordnance which had been removed from operational men-of-war at Chatham. She was laid up in 1672 and sold out of the service eleven years later, in 1683.

At about the time of the Civil War, and during the early part of the Commonwealth, more *Eagles* saw service. The first of these was a 6-gun shallop which was used for guard duties in the Channel. The second was a 150-ton frigate with 12 guns which was originally captured from the French, and she was hired by the Commonwealth in 1650. In September 1652 she took part in the battle of Kentish Knock in the Anglo-Dutch War, and saw action off Portland between 18 and 21 February 1653, when the English fleet under Blake and Monk defeated a Dutch fleet under Van Trump. In July the same year she took part in the two-day battle near the Gabbard, and the resulting victory gave command of the seas to England. She was returned to her owners in 1655, at the end of the war.

The next *Eagle* appears to have been a 300-ton fifth-rate armed with 22 guns. She was built at Wapping in 1654 as the *Selby*, commemorating a Parliamentary victory in the Civil War. However, in 1660, after the Restoration, she was renamed *Eagle*. She saw service in the West Indies, but in April 1665, after the outbreak of the second Dutch War, she formed part of a fleet blockading the Zuyder Zee. In June the same year she was present when the Duke of York was victorious off Lowestoft. In 1674 she was converted for use as a fireship, but she was never used as such and in 1688 she was put to use as a guardship at Sheerness. Six years later, in 1694, she was sunk to form a breakwater at the same port.

In those times fireships were widely used in sea warfare, being fearsome weapons which caused confusion and panic. They were also a sure way of destroying wooden ships of the period. One such 240-ton, six-gun vessel was captured from the Dutch in 1666 and expended as a fireship in the four-day battle of 1-4 June 1666 off Orfordness. Another was a 50-ton, six-gun ship captured from Algerian pirates in 1670, and she was needlessly expended in the following year, on 2 May 1671, in the unsuccessful night attack on the pirate stronghold of Bugia Bay (Bougie). The third fireship, named *Eagle*, was a 208-ton vessel which was purchased in 1672, but which foundered in April the following year whilst on passage to St Helena.

The next *Eagle* was a 1,047-ton third-rate with 70 guns, built at Portsmouth in 1679. She was 120 feet long with a beam of 40 feet, and a complement of 460 officers and men. For the first ten years of her career she was laid up in reserve, but in 1689, after England entered into an alliance with Holland and Austria in a war against France, she was brought to operational readiness. In May 1692 she formed part of Admiral Russell's fleet in the decisive defeat of the French off Barfleur. Four days later, flying the flag of Admiral Sir George Rooke, she led the force which attacked the remnants of the French fleet which was sheltering at La Hogue. The French ships were anchored close inshore and it was decided to cut them out with the ship's boats. On the night of 23 May six ships were burnt and the following morning a further four were destroyed. The water was so shallow that at one time the boats had to repel a charge by French cavalrymen. In 1699 the *Eagle* was rebuilt at Chatham and three years later, in August 1702, she took part in Admiral Rooke's abortive attack on Cadiz. She also formed part of his fleet in July 1704, at the capture of Gibraltar. In the following month, on 13 August, she expended all her powder and shot and suffered heavy casualties in the battle of Velez Malaga. This action ensured that the French Toulon fleet was decisively beaten, and it did not venture out of the port again for the rest of the war. After this battle the *Eagle* remained in the Mediterranean where she was employed in support of the army on the Spanish coast. On 23 September 1705 she was present during the bombardment of Barcelona and in October 1707, as part of a squadron under Admiral Sir Cloudesly Shovell, she sailed for home waters. However, on 22 October, she was wrecked off the Scilly Islands in thick fog, going down with the loss of all hands, including Admiral Shovell.

Another *Eagle* listed in the records was a 150-ton, 10-gun vessel built at Arundel in 1696. She was employed in the Channel until 27 November 1703 when she was wrecked on the Sussex coast.

The next recorded *Eagle* was a 60-gun fourth-rate of 1,130 tons which was launched in December 1744 at Portsmouth as the *Centurian*, but commissioned as the *Eagle* in 1745. By this time England was once again at war with France and the *Eagle* came under the command of Captain G. B. Rodney, who later became the famous Admiral. In October 1746 she fought and captured the Spanish privateer *Esperanza* and a French vessel, the *Shoreham* (formerly seized from the British). In June 1747 she formed part of Commodore Fox's squadron which overpowered a convoy of 50 French West Indiamen, valued at over £1 million. In the following month, in company with the *Edinburgh* and *Nottingham*, she captured the 36-gun French privateer, *Bellone*, which later served in the Royal Navy as the *Bellona*. On 14 October 1747 she was present at Hawke's encounter off Ushant with *L'Etenduere*, which was escorting an outward-bound convoy of 252 West Indiamen.

One of her ship's company during this action was Able Seaman James Cook who later rose to the rank of captain. In March 1748 the *Eagle* was part of a squadron which captured a Spanish convoy off Cape Cantin in Morocco, and that was the last action she saw before paying off in August that year at the end of the war.

However, the peace did not last and the *Eagle* was recommissioned in 1756 at the start of the Seven Years' War. Her only action in this war was in the Channel on 30 May 1757 when, in company with the *Medway*, she defeated the heavily armed French privateer *Duc d' Acquitaine*. In 1758 the *Eagle* lost her masts during a hurricane off the American coast, but she managed to limp back to England where she was paid off and used as a hulk until she was finally sold for £600 in 1767.

Very little is known of the next *Eagle* other than she was a Bombay Marine cruiser of eight guns, built in the Indian city in 1754.

The next *Eagle* was a third-rate of 1,372 tons, armed with 60 guns, which was launched on the Thames in 1774. She had a complement of 522 officers and men and she was first commissioned in February 1776. From July that year until September 1778 she was Admiral Lord Howe's flagship on the North American Station while the American colonies were waging their successful war for independence. In October 1777 a remarkable attempt was made by the Americans to blow up the *Eagle* as she lay at anchor off Grosvenor's Island, in the Hudson River, using a hand-propelled, one-man submarine. However, the inventor, David Bushnell, was taken ill at the last moment and his replacement, although a brave man, was not very skilled at handling the strange craft. He was detected before he reached the *Eagle* so he abandoned the 'submarine' some distance from the ship and it did no damage when it blew up. In 1778 France entered the war on the American side and the *Eagle* was present at Howe's successful defence of New York against a superior French fleet. In September 1778 she returned to England and after a refit she went out to India as part of a squadron commanded by Admiral Sir Edward Hughes. She saw little action until 1782 when she won honours against a French squadron, under the command of Vice-Admiral Suffren, at Sadras, Providien, Negapatam and Trincomalee. The *Eagle* returned home to Chatham in 1786 and was paid off, not returning to service until 1794 when she was fitted out as a hospital ship. However, this role did not last long and in 1797, renamed *Buckingham*, she was converted to a prison ship. Many of the men who were court-martialled after the Nore mutiny served their sentences in her. In 1812 she was broken up at the ripe old age of 38.

During the time the last *Eagle* was at Chatham, two gunboats named *Eagle* served with the Royal Navy. The first was a 71-ton, four-gun vessel which was bought in 1794 and sold in 1802. The second, a vessel of 158 tons, armed with 12 guns, was captured from the French in 1803 as the *La Ventura* and renamed *Eagle*. However, in the following year she was renamed *Eclipse* as the name *Eagle* was required for a new vessel which was building at Northfleet.

This *Eagle* was a third-rate of 1,723 tons, armed with 74 guns, which had been laid down at Northfleet in 1800 and which was launched on 27 February 1804. At this time the Napoleonic War was entering its second phase and the threat of invasion lay over the British Isles, with our fleets busy blockading the coast of Europe. In 1804, flying the flag of Rear-Admiral Thornbrough, she took part in the blockade of the Texel. In January 1805 she was with Cornwallis blockading Brest and in April she was with Rear-Admiral Cochrane's squadron chasing French Rochefort ships. Later that year, after Nelson's great victory at Trafalgar, the threat of invasion was removed and the *Eagle* was transferred to the Mediterranean. In May 1806 she was part of Admiral Sir Sydney Smith's squadron when the seamen and marines of the fleet were landed to take the Island of Capri, and later she assisted at the defence of Gaeta. After being present at Collingwood's blockading of Toulon in 1807 and 1808, she returned home and took part in Lord Chatham's Walcheron Expedition to capture Antwerp. This, however, proved to be a very expensive exercise and it was abandoned. In 1810, on her way to join the Mediterranean Fleet, she assisted in the defence of Cadiz against Marshal Soult. On arrival in the Mediterranean she was allocated duties in the Adriatic where her exploits included the capture of the French frigate *Corcyre* as well as numerous merchantmen, and the destruction of shore batteries at Coste, Farasina and Omago. In July 1813 she was present at the capture of Fiume, with her landing parties being led by her captain, and in August she was at the capture of Rovigno where 21 store ships were seized. In October that year she was present at the capture of Trieste, but soon after this she returned home and was paid off for an extensive refit. The war ended before this was completed and she was laid up until 1832, when she entered service with the coastguard at Falmouth and Milford Haven. In 1860 she became a drill ship in Southampton Water and two years later she went to Liverpool as the drill ship for the RNR. She continued in this role until 1910 when she was transferred to the RNVR and in 1918, when the name *Eagle* was required for a new aircraft carrier, the old ship was renamed *Eaglet*. She was finally broken up in 1926.

Appendix Four

HMS *Eagle* 1913-1942

In 1913 the government of Chile ordered a dreadnought battleship from the Tyneside shipbuilding company of Armstrong Whitworth & Co, and the company's naval architects designed the vessel which was to have been named *Almirante Cochrane*. On the outbreak of the Great War in August 1914 work on the battleship, which had been virtually completed up to forecastle deck, was stopped. Her main machinery, which consisted of 32 Yarrow coal-fired boilers and four sets of geared turbines, had been fitted, but her side armour had not. For over three years the uncompleted hull of the dreadnought lay on the slipway as the company's, and the nation's, priorities turned to the construction of British ships.

Meanwhile, naval aviation had been making rapid progress and in the spring of 1913 the Admiralty decided to convert the almost completed light battlecruiser HMS *Furious* to an aircraft carrier. This vessel was actually in Armstrong's fitting-out basin at the time, and the after 18-inch gun turret had been installed, although the forward turret was still under construction. At this stage the design was altered and the forward turret was dispensed with and replaced by a sloped flying-off deck, which extended over the forecastle, and an aircraft hangar. The vessel was completed to this design in the summer of 1917 and she then joined the fleet. However, this arrangement did not prove satisfactory and later that year she was returned to her builders for the removal of the 18-inch gun at the stern and for the construction of a flight deck aft of the funnel, together with a large hangar beneath it. This design, although an improvement on the original, was still not ideal since only a large gantry with vertical cables suspended from it prevented aircraft from hitting the funnel when landing on from aft. By this time the Admiralty had finalized plans for a vessel with a completely flat flight deck from stem to stern, with a raised island superstructure on the starboard side which would house the navigating bridge, the mast and the funnels, as funnel gases which caused draughts and eddies over the after landing deck of the *Furious* had been another problem. The uncompleted hull of the *Almirante Cochrane* was the answer and on the last day of February 1918 the Admiralty purchased it from the Chilean government for £1,334,358 and renamed it HMS *Eagle*.

The new ship was launched on 8 June 1918 by the wife of the United States Ambassador, but following the Armistice in November 1918 the shipyard was plagued by industrial disputes and so, in March 1920, as she had been completed sufficiently for her to be moved down to Portsmouth where she could undergo trials, she put to sea for the first time for her passage south. On this voyage she had only one funnel (a limited number of boilers were working), no mast, and a temporary wooden structure on the island to serve as the navigating bridge. She had accommodation for just over 400 men. Once she arrived at Portsmouth, despite the fact that she was far from complete, flying trials were carried out to test different types of arrester gear and to familiarize pilots with landing techniques. It also had to be ascertained whether this 667ft carrier, with its large island superstructure on the starboard side, could launch and land aircraft safely. The unit chosen to carry out these trials was No 444 (RAF) Fleet Reconnaissance Flight, and they quickly got used to operating from the ship.

The *Eagle* in 1919 as she left the River Tyne. She has only one funnel and a temporary wooden bridge.
(*Maritime Photo Library*)

The initial trials were completed in October 1920 and the *Eagle* then paid off at Devonport Dockyard. In March 1921 work on her began again at Portsmouth and lasted for two and a half years. During this time some major modernization work was carried out including the conversion of the boilers from coal to oil-burning and the fitting of more up-to-date armament. The work was completed in the autumn of 1923 and the final cost, including her purchase from the Chilean government, amounted to £4,617,636. After carrying out her sea trials the *Eagle* eventually commissioned in February 1924, after which she joined the Mediterranean Fleet at Malta.

In 1927 she went to Venice to act as a base for the RAF Flight which won the Schneider Cup and in June 1929, while on passage to Gibraltar, she was diverted from her course to look for a missing Spanish seaplane. The Dornier flying boat was being flown by Major Ramon Franco, the brother of Generalissimo Franco who would eventually rule Spain from 1939 to 1975. The plane had left Cartagena, bound for the Azores, at 5pm on 21 June and it had passed Cape St Vincent four hours later. The pilot then was forced to gain height owing to turbulence and he ended up with his aircraft sandwiched between two layers of cloud. They had been due to arrive in the Azores at 9am on 22 June, but a strong north-easterly wind caused them to pass over the islands and completely miss their destination during the night, and when they were able to check their position they found that they were too far south-west. In order to economize on fuel and to check their position more accurately, Major Franco landed the aircraft on the sea and, when they had obtained an accurate fix, he took off once more. However, strong headwinds slowed the aircraft down and it ran out of fuel some 40 miles from Fayal. Fortunately, he was able to land safely, but the strong winds caused the aircraft to drift and by the following day it was about 100 miles from Fayal. On 24 June gale force winds got up and by 27 June the situation had become extremely dangerous.

Meanwhile the *Eagle*, which had been searching for some days and which had been hampered by bad weather, finally found the flying boat in the vicinity of the island of Santa Maria at dawn on 29 June and took all the grateful occupants of the Dornier on board. Apparently the Spanish Press had already decided that the Dornier and its passengers were lost for good and the news that they had been rescued caused great celebrations throughout Spain. The captain and officers of the *Eagle* were invited to dine with King Alfonso of Spain and a Spanish nobleman, the Duke of Alba, presented a 32in-high silver model of an eagle to the ship. When war broke out in 1939 the model was stored ashore, and in 1952 it was transferred to the wardroom of the 21st *Eagle* where it was considered to be one of the most valuable pieces in the ship's collection.

In 1931, accompanied by the destroyer *Achates*, the *Eagle* visited South America for the British Empire Trade Exhibition at Buenos Aires, which was opened by the Prince of Wales. The *Eagle's* aircraft gave flying displays at both Buenos Aires and Rio de Janeiro, and then on her return to the UK later that year she was taken in hand for a major refit at Devonport. In March 1933, with the work completed, she was sent to the China Station and in the following year her aircraft located and forced the surrender of Chinese pirates who had seized and looted the steamer *Shuntien* and who were holding several of her passengers for ransom in a hideout near the Yellow River.

The *Eagle* returned home in 1935 and was put in reserve until January 1937 when she was again commissioned for service on the China Station. When the Second World War broke out in September 1939 she was refitting in the newly opened Naval Base at Singapore and her strike force at this time consisted of 17 Fairey Swordfish torpedo bombers.

In this unusual view looking forward, the Royal Marines Band is playing just aft of the island on the flight deck while the *Eagle* is manoeuvred to her berth in Malta's Grand Harbour. (*M. Cassar*)

Following the refit she was transferred to Trincomalee, Ceylon (Sri Lanka), and in the summer of 1940 she made her northbound transit of the Suez Canal and arrived at Alexandria on 9 June 1940, to join Admiral Cunningham's Mediterranean Fleet. Four days later she was at sea with the fleet and her aircraft were in action as they attacked Italian shipping. It was a very busy period for the ship and her squadrons as they were used to harry the North African ports, often from improvised bases in the desert. *Eagle* was present at the Battle of Calabria on 9 July 1940 when her Swordfish flew reconnaissance missions for most of the day, and put in two air strikes on Italian ships, torpedoing a cruiser in the second of these. A defect in her petrol system prevented her from taking part in the attack on Taranto, but five of her aircraft and eight aircrew were embarked in the *Illustrious* for this successful operation. On 22 August 1940 her aircraft took part in a night attack on Bomba, when three Swordfish sank two large submarines, a destroyer and a depot ship with only three torpedoes. However, by January 1941 she was long overdue for a refit and in April that year she passed south through the Suez Canal and returned home by way of Cape Town.

By early 1942 she was operational once again and based on Gibraltar where she was principally employed in escorting convoys to Malta. In February she and the USS *Wasp* carried 70 Spitfires to a position where they could fly to Malta. Between February and July she made nine such ferrying trips and dispatched 183 Spitfires to the island. In August 1942 a major effort was made to relieve the beleaguered garrison of Malta, with 14 valuable merchant ships carrying vital stores, together with a heavy escort which included the cruisers *Cairo* and *Manchester*. There were also four aircraft carriers, the *Indomitable*, *Victorious* and *Eagle*, which between them carried 72 fighters mainly for convoy protection, and the *Furious*, which carried 38 Spitfires for the island. There were also two battleships, *Nelson* and *Rodney*, together with 15 destroyers. The convoy left Gibraltar on 9 August and two days later the Allied ships were at full alert for air attacks which it was anticipated would be launched from Sardinia and Sicily. Four Sea Hurricanes from the *Eagle* and four from the *Victorious* were aloft on patrol when, at about 1.15pm, four terrific explosions were seen on the *Eagle's* port side. The first torpedo had struck the *Eagle's* port quarter and this was followed by three more in quick succession. A news correspondent who was on board at the time reported that: 'Terrific explosions shook the ship from stem to stem.' After the first hit the carrier heeled five degrees to port and this quickly increased to fifteen degrees. All the explosions were in the area of the ship's port machinery spaces and the resultant flooding was rapid and extremely serious. On board one of the merchantmen one of the lookouts recalled: 'I was astounded at the sight of the two-funnelled carrier *Eagle* apparently turning so sharply that she was heeling over.' This witness recalls a destroyer racing over towards the carrier and the 'unthinkable' dawning on him as the *Eagle*, '...was turning on her side and aircraft were sliding into the sea from the flight deck.' He went on to say, 'I could not resist watching the *Eagle*, but I did not see her for long because apart from the fact that she was dropping astern, she was also sinking fast.'

The *Eagle* sank within ten minutes of being hit and 160 members of her ship's company were lost. Other losses as a result of 'Operation Pedestal' included the cruisers *Cairo* and *Manchester*, and the destroyer *Foresight*, and of the 14 merchantmen only five made it to Malta.

The *Eagle* high and dry in a floating dry dock during the 1930s.
(*Maritime Photo Library*)

At sea off Gibraltar. *(Fleet Air Arm Museum)*

HMS *Eagle* in 1939. *(Maritime Photo Library)*

HMS *Eagle*
Arduus ad Solem
(By Labour To The Sun)

Battle Honours:

Portland	1653	Ushant	1747
Gabbard	1653	Sadras	1782
Lowestoft	1665	Provedien	1782
Orfordness	1666	Negapatam	1782
Barfleur	1692	Trincomalee	1782
Gibraltar	1704	Calabria	1940
Velez Malaga	1704	Mediterranean	1940
	Malta Convoys	1942	

Acknowledgements:

My thanks to Rear-Admiral I. G. W. Robertson CB DSC, the *Eagle's* last Commanding Officer, for kindly writing the foreword to this book. To Lady D. E. Holland-Martin OBE for her help and for the loan of her photograph albums. To Admiral Sir John Roxburgh KCB CBE DSO DSC for his valuable assistance with diary excerpts. To Captain Hugh Owen RN (Retd) and to Admiral Sir John Treacher KCB for their help.

I must also thank the following for their help and, in many cases, for the loan of very valuable photographs:-

Jim Allaway, Editor, *Navy News*: Kenneth Anderson, Ulster Folk & Transport Museum: George Austin: Michael Axford: Mrs Sheila Ballantyne, *The Echo*, Southampton: Roger Beacham and staff, Cheltenham Reference Library: M. L. Burns: Michael Cassar, Valletta, Malta: Norman F. Curnow: Sydney Dean: W. J. R. Dite: J. A. Donaldson: Digby Forster: Peter Harris: Terry Heaps: Morris Holm: Richard Holme: Patrick Horan: Paul Hurley: Mrs Brenda Jacob, *The News*, Portsmouth: Ian Johnston: Michael Kettle: Peter Legg: Terence G. Lelliott: R. Selwyn Maund: Aubrey C. A. Moore: L. K. Moore: John Neil, Editor, *Wigtown Free Press*: Michael D. Pack: M. K. Pagan: N. E. D. Parkinson, HMS *Bulwark* Association: Anthony J. Perrett: W. J. Pilgrim: K. J. Pitchford: David Richardson, Research Officer, Fleet Air Arm Museum: Kenneth W. Rimmer: N. Sims: J. A. Slater: John Solway, Imperial War Museum: Ian Spashett, FotoFlite: Mrs Kathleen Stickland: Adrian Vicary, Maritime Photo Library:

Special thanks to Mr Brian Conroy, Whitehill, Hampshire, for the watercolour painting of HMS *Eagle* used on the front cover.

Also In The Series

HMS *Albion* 1944-1973 The Old Grey Ghost   £13.95
(Plus £1.50 p&p in UK/EU or £3.50 for airmail to all other countries)

Available From:
FAN PUBLICATIONS
17 Wymans Lane
Cheltenham
Glos GL51 9QA
England
Tel/Fax: 01242 580290